House Beautiful

DESIGN & DECORATE
LIVING & DINING ROOMS

House Beautiful

DESIGN & DECORATE
LIVING & DINING ROOMS

Creating Beautiful Rooms
from Start to Finish

TESSA EVELEGH

HEARST BOOKS
A division of Sterling Publishing Co., Inc.

New York / London

Created, edited, and designed by
Duncan Baird Publishers Ltd.,
Castle House, 75–76 Wells Street, London W1T 3QH

Managing Editor: Emma Callery
Designer: Alison Shackleton
Illustrator: Kate Simunek

Library of Congress Cataloging-in-Publication Data

Evelegh, Tessa.
  House beautiful design & decorate : living and dining rooms : creating beautiful rooms from start to finish / Tessa Evelegh.
      p. cm.
  Includes index.
  ISBN-13: 978-1-58816-651-7
  ISBN-10: 1-58816-651-1
  1. Living rooms. 2. Dining rooms. 3. Interior decoration. I. House beautiful. II. Title. III. Title: House beautiful design and decorate. IV. Title: Design & decorate : living and dining rooms.
  NK2117.L5E94 2007
  747.7'5--dc22

                        2007007272

1 2 3 4 5 6 7 8 9 10

Published by Hearst Books
A Division of Sterling Publishing Co., Inc.
387 Park Avenue South, New York, NY 10016

House Beautiful and Hearst Books are trademarks of Hearst Communications, Inc.

www.housebeautiful.com

For information about custom editions, special sales, premium and corporate purchases, please contact Sterling Special Sales Department at 800-805-5489 or specialsales@sterlingpub.com.

Distributed in Canada by Sterling Publishing
Canadian Manda Group, 165 Dufferin Street
Toronto, Ontario, Canada M6K 3H6

Distributed in Australia by Capricorn Link
(Australia) Pty. Ltd.
P.O. Box 704, Windsor, NSW 2756 Australia

Manufactured in China

Sterling ISBN 13: 978-1-58816-651-7
        ISBN 10: 1-58816-651-1

CONTENTS

6

Foreword

Living rooms and dining rooms are your own personal retreat. Make them yours, make them beautiful, and make them work for you and your family. That's a tall order—home life just isn't so simple these days. Living rooms are no longer formal parlors. They now have to accommodate the TV at the least, or home theater at the most, possibly together with separate sound systems, game players, and all the related media, books, personal memorabilia, and accessories. The dining room might be separate, but then again, it might not be.

Somehow, the simple, traditional living rooms and dining rooms no longer quite fit the bill, and many of us are just making do. It's not necessarily about throwing out all the old and starting from scratch, but if you're planning on redesigning and/or redecorating these rooms, now could be just the time for a major rethink. And that's what this book is about. It will help you answer the questions: "What suits us right now?" and "How can we make this work for us?" in terms of style and lifestyle, both of which are very likely to have changed since you last redecorated.

The book is divided into two sections. The first, "Design," is about evaluating your lifestyle, carefully planning, and making any necessary changes to the structure, fixtures, and major pieces of furniture within the rooms. All of this is worth thinking through, even if it's only to ensure you're happy with the way things are. Then you'll be ready to embark on the decorating and finishing touches—the "Decorate" part of the book—such as choosing colors, fabrics, and accessories. Filled with inspirational images, *Design and Decorate* is also packed with useful information, all aimed at helping you think through the best solutions for fabulous living and dining rooms that perfectly suit your lifestyle.

The Editors of *House Beautiful*

be prepared

Purists would say that the design process starts with assessing your lifestyle and doesn't finish until the last table lamp has been plugged in and the final pillows scattered. But for the purposes of this book, the design part focuses on the long term: the planning and the permanent elements of the interior design process, rather than the finishes. As with any project, putting in time at this stage always pays off.

ABOVE: TELEVISION SCREENS HAVE TAKEN OVER FROM FIREPLACES AS THE MOST POPULAR FOCAL POINT.

OPPOSITE: FOR DINING ROOMS, PRIORITIZE SCALE SO THAT THE FURNITURE IS IN PROPORTION TO THE ROOM'S DIMENSIONS.

This is where you do your thinking, research your options, and make your decisions. The more energy you put into this, the more you are likely to be delighted with the end result. This planning will probably have more positive impact on your everyday life than you could possibly have imagined. It could also be that this planning stage will save money in the long run. Having put in lots of thought, you're less likely to change your mind (which is always costly, especially once the work has started), and more likely to have hunted down the bargains.

This section of the book aims to be instructive, whether you plan to do-it-yourself or whether you want to be prepared with a well-thought-out brief, ready for when you call in the professionals. Well-planned doesn't have to cost any more, but it will have a positive effect on the design of the room, the way you use it and, ultimately, on your sense of well-being.

Know your style

Enthusiasm for the initial vision of your renovated living room has to be the fuel that kick-starts the job. It also has to be what keeps you going through the months ahead as you realize your dream. But the initial vision depends on having a strong sense of style. Even if you're building on what you already have and simply want to update with fresh wall colors or an interesting wall covering, you'll need to put in some research on what is available in the stores right now. If you're starting from scratch, because, for example, you've moved in with a new partner and you need to do a bit of design match-making, or because you've moved into a new house of a different period, you'll want to spend considerably more time thinking about what you like. Only when you're sure you adore something will it be the right time to buy. So how do you begin?

- **You may be inspired by something you've seen** in a friend's house or at an interior design store. It might be a wonderful color combination, a fabulous piece of fabric, or even a stunning piece of furniture.

- **Cut out photographs** of rooms and pieces of furniture that please you from magazines, and visit a few of your favorite home furnishing stores to see what's available right now—take snapshots if you can, or pick up any relevant catalogs.

- **Mount all your carefully collected references** onto a board, or make up a file divided into sections on whole rooms, furniture, accessories, lighting, etc., to build up an overall picture of all the things you like best. You might find a file more practical to use than a board, partly because it's more portable, and partly because later on down the line, you'll be able to add information, such as the exact dimensions of a sofa you've sourced, or a fabric swatch plus name, colorway, and repeat.

In your enthusiasm, don't feel you necessarily have to throw everything out. Many of the best interiors are the result of happy accidents where an old favorite textile, for example, juxtaposed with something new, finds fresh life. Sometimes colors you'd never have thought of putting together take on a vibrancy you couldn't have imagined. This is the way to progress from a particular style to developing one all of your own.

ABOVE: TRADITIONAL SCANDINAVIAN STYLE HAS AN ELEGANCE THAT TRANSCENDS TIME, AS DEMONSTRATED BY THIS ATTRACTIVE LIVING ROOM.

OPPOSITE: RE-THINKING YOUR ROOM DOESN'T NECESSARILY MEAN THROWING OUT ALL THE OLD. FAMILY FAVORITES CAN TEAM HAPPILY WITH NEWER PURCHASES IF THEY HAVE A STYLE LINK AND ARE OF A SIMILAR SCALE.

assess your lifestyle

It's not difficult to see why many of us are tempted to simply make do with the furnishings we have in the space available to us. Neither decorating nor furnishings come cheap and since we don't make over our living and dining rooms on a regular basis, few people have the confidence to strike out with a completely new vision.

However, there are times and situations when it makes sense to start with a clean slate and take a cool new look at your space and how it is working for you, with regard both to your current lifestyle and how you think it is likely to change in the not-too-distant future. For you, that time might be when you've just moved; when the room looks tired and is in need of a fresh look; when the children have moved on to a different stage; or when the technology is dated. Home theater systems and flat and plasma screens impact on the interior design of the room and have different space needs than old-fashioned tube televisions. The same goes for new-generation sound systems.

Early in the twentieth century it was the father of architectural modernism, Louis Henri Sullivan, who popularized the notion that "form follows function." It's still a very liberating maxim, even within the domestic situation. Instead of making do with what is there, before you even begin to look at design details, think about how the space would function best for your lifestyle. This will inform the finished design and help immensely both when you come to consulting professionals and selecting furniture. Thinking through your space as if you're starting from scratch may sound drastic, but it needn't be. It's not necessarily about discarding everything you already have, it's more about assessing exactly what you need for your lifestyle, and then coming up with a solution that may well incorporate much of what you already have. Alternatively, you may well find that your family has outgrown certain items or arrangements, which are now proving to be more of an impediment than an aid to relaxation.

ABOVE: IF YOU LOVE BIG GET-TOGETHERS, PLAN FOR AS MUCH EXTRA SEATING AS YOU CAN. THIS BUILT-IN WINDOW SEAT ENHANCES THE ARCHITECTURE AND PROVIDES COMFORTABLE PLACES FOR TWO.

OPPOSITE: CONSIDER UPWARD MOVES AS THE FAMILY GROWS. THIS ATTIC EXTENSION PROVIDES A CLEAN, MODERN LIVING ROOM FOR OLDER TEENAGERS OR STUDENTS—OR A PEACEFUL OASIS FOR YOURSELVES.

Get going

So how do you go about assessing your lifestyle? It all comes down to being honest with yourself, letting go of what you no longer need, retaining what you need now, and projecting forward, probably five years, to assess what the family may need then.

BELOW LEFT: SOCIALIZING WITH FRIENDS DOES NOT NECESSARILY REQUIRE ACCESS TO HOME ENTERTAINMENT SYSTEMS. WELL-PLANNED SEATING IS OFTEN ALL YOU NEED.

BELOW RIGHT: PLANNING THE SEATING HAS TO RELATE TO THE POSITION OF THE TV SCREEN IF EVERYONE IS GOING TO GET A GOOD VIEW.

OPPOSITE: IF YOU DON'T HAVE SPACE FOR A SINGLE-USE DINING ROOM, THINK MULTIFUNCTION. THE TABLE IN THIS GARDEN ROOM DOUBLES UP FOR DINING.

• **List the current activities** that take place in the room. Discard any of the functions you may now recognize as belonging to the past.

• **Project forward** by allowing for activities the children may want in five years' time. For example, computer games may soon be replacing building blocks.

• **Consider the storage** to accommodate those activities, such as for CDs, DVDs, computers, and games.

• **Plan the furniture.** Do you need more seating space or more activity space?

• **Think about the space.** Do you want to see from one room to another so you can keep an eye on the children, or do you want to hide toys while you entertain?

• **Consider the TV/home theater.** Is it time you changed the technology? How big is the equipment likely to be? Will it be the focal point of the room? If so, how will that affect the rest of the furniture and its arrangement?

ABOVE: LIGHT, AIRY SPACES
WHERE THERE IS NO NEED FOR
A TELEVISION, ARE EXCELLENT FOR
SOCIALIZING AS THE SEATING
ARRANGEMENT DOES NOT NEED TO
BE LIMITED BY THE POSITION OF
THE TELEVISION.

OPPOSITE: BY WALL-MOUNTING
THE TV SCREEN, YOU CAN
DISPENSE WITH SPACE-HUNGRY
MEDIA STANDS. POSITIONED ABOVE
THE FIREPLACE, THERE'S A SINGLE
FOCAL POINT IN THE ROOM, WHICH
MEANS THE FURNITURE CAN BE
MORE STREAMLINED IN ITS
POSITIONING.

Living rooms

Here's an example of completely rethinking your living room. It could be that you were brought up in a traditional house that incorporated a family living room and a "parlor," which was kept pristine for receiving guests. This may seem like an unnecessary waste of space in today's less formal society, so instead, you may decide to use one room for the television and home entertainment, and equip another with the sound system for relaxing with friends. Another family may prefer to join the two rooms into one large area to make better use of the available light and space. Yet another solution would be to open up the space but divide it again using sliding doors for ultimate flexibility—open plan some of the time, divided at others.

The whole issue of modern technology could be the very reason many people want to rethink the living room. A large flat TV screen with its attendant stands and storage furniture has a completely different impact on the interior design of the living room than an old-fashioned tube television. If you go for a plasma screen, that challenge will be completely different as it could be installed into the wall, possibly at a high level, freeing up the whole arrangement of the room.

Another reason for change could be changing seating needs. A family consisting of parents plus two toddlers have very different needs to a family that includes teens and their friends. Suddenly, the sofa seems far too small to accommodate the growing crowd, yet the room isn't any larger. The solution could be as simple as re-hanging the door so it opens a different way, thereby creating more space within the room. Alternatively, now you no longer need toddler play-space, you may be able to use more of the room for sofas and other seating, replacing a traditional three-seater with a roomy six-seat corner design that teens love for lounging.

Once you've outlined the main functions, you need to consider any support roles for them. You'll need to think about:
• **CD and possibly vinyl storage** near the sound system.
• **Space for DVDs and game players** near the television or home theater.
• **Display space for books,** family photographs, and accessories.
• **Whether you'd prefer built-in storage** or if freestanding storage furniture may be more suitable for your lifestyle. Freestanding often gives a younger, more carefree look to the room, but whatever your age and style, it may be right for you, if, for example, you're likely to be moving in the not-too-distant future and you'd like to take your investment with you.

Dining rooms

The function of single-use dining rooms is clearly far less complicated than those of modern open-plan living rooms. The minimum furniture that a dining room needs is a table and chairs. If you're tight on space, bear in mind that you'll need at least three feet between the fully extended table's edge and the wall to allow for pull-back space for the chairs. If you have space, a side table provides both decorative interest to the room and a useful surface for serving.

You will also need to think about your storage needs, which, at most, would include space for china, glass, table linens, flatware, candles, and candlesticks. These can either be kept in the dining room where they will be used, or in the kitchen where they will be washed. The choice will depend on the available space in your dining room,

BELOW LEFT: AN OVAL TABLE MAKES EFFICIENT USE OF SPACE AND OFFERS A PLEASING CONTRAST IN A RECTANGULAR ROOM.

BELOW RIGHT: AN EXTENDABLE DINING TABLE IS AN EXCELLENT CHOICE WHERE SPACE IS TIGHT. KEEP IT SMALL MOST OF THE TIME AND EXTEND IT ONLY WHEN YOU ARE ENTERTAINING.

the proximity to the kitchen, and how frequently you use the dining room. It may also depend on whether or not you have only "everyday" china, glass, and cutlery, or whether you also have "best." If "everyday" is your style (whatever the occasion), then you may like to keep everything in the kitchen as it will always need to be washed, and, presumably, sometimes used there, too.

If, however, you do have china, glass, and flatware reserved for special occasions, you may well want to store them in the dining room, well away from the hustle and bustle of the kitchen where they may be damaged. All this might seem like small detail, but it can impact on the ergonomics of the space, making a big difference in the time you spend in preparation and clearing up.

WHERE THERE'S SPACE, ALLOW FOR A SIDE TABLE FOR SERVING PLUS STORAGE FOR CHINA, GLASS, AND FLATWARE.

Multifunction dining rooms

In many houses, a single-use dining room is a luxury, and you may like to put the dining space to multifunctional use. For example, you may like to transform the room into a playroom, workroom, or office during the day. This could affect both the colors you use and furniture you choose. A neat gate-leg table that folds down to next-to-nothing could be useful teamed with folding or stacking chairs if you need to clear the floor space for a playroom.

Alternatively, you may prefer to transform the dining room into an efficient home office during the day. A laptop computer could be used on any table—solid, drop-leaf, or leaf-extendable—while, if there is space, the room could be furnished with an all-in-one cabinet for files and paperwork that can be closed up at the end of the day. Another idea would be to have closets running floor to ceiling the full length of one wall, which could be used partly for dining needs, and partly for toys or office files and stationery, depending on how you are using the room.

Living-dining rooms

More and more modern homes have open-plan living-dining rooms, which can bring a greater sense of space and light than those that are divided. Without walls, the divide between living and dining can find its own place, allowing the seating area, for example, to expand beyond where the walls would have been, while dining furniture can be folded down or stacked up when not in use. Open-plan living also results in a much lighter and airier feel to the space as the natural light travels unhindered from one space to the next. In cooler climates, previous generations avoided open-plan living in an attempt to conserve heat during the winter months. Today, double- and triple-glazed windows and central heating have solved that issue, and embracing plenty of natural light has become much more of a priority.

Another advantage of open plan is that if the space is looked at as a whole, then some of its functions, such as storage, can be shared. A single long expanse of floor-to-ceiling cabinets that rob very little space from the floor area, for example, can be so discreet as to almost give the appearance of a wall, while providing a huge amount of storage for both rooms. Even in traditional homes, a long wall of closets can look beautiful, especially if the doors are paneled in keeping with the rest of the architecture and finished with elegant handles or knobs.

You may decide to leave the living and dining space completely open, with one end of the room devoted to relaxing, flowing into a dining area at the other unhindered by any boundaries. Or you may prefer to screen off one area from the other. You could do this by:

• **Using traditional folding screens,** which can be moved about, fully opened out, partly folded or even removed, depending on the circumstances.

• **Suspending simple fabric panels** from rails fastened to the ceiling. If you run the rails the full width of the room, the panels can then be drawn along them to screen off different parts of the room as desired. You could create even more interest by installing two rails parallel to each other across the width of the space. That way, several decorative panels can be hung on each rail, overlapping in front of and behind each other to create a changing wall of fabric. If the fabrics are sheer, you could use different-colored ones so the shades blend in different ways, depending on which hues are overlapped.

• **Incorporating freestanding open bookshelves** into your design. This has the practical advantage of providing storage and display space that can be used from both sides.

• **Installing sliding doors,** which is a more solid, architectural solution. Use them to completely close off one part of the living-dining room from the other, so they can be closed when you want privacy, or left open for a more airy feel.

IF YOU HAVE A LARGE SPACE, THEN OPEN-PLAN LIVING CAN BE THE WAY TO GO—ESPECIALLY IF YOU DON'T NEED TO EVEN TEMPORARILY DIVIDE THE SPACE. IN THIS AIRY ROOM, THE LIVING AND DINING AREA HAS BEEN SEPARATED FROM THE KITCHEN BY A PERMANENT STRUCTURE THAT CREATES A ROOM WITHIN A ROOM.

plan the layout

Inspired, well-planned interiors not only look good, they also make the very best use of space and are generally the most comfortable to live in. It's at this very early stage in the design process that you need to consider the complete picture. You've already thought through your lifestyle, wishes, and needs, now look at the architecture of your room and consider whether or not you'd like to make any structural changes; whether radiators, electrical outlets, and lighting fixtures (see pages 36–49) are where you want them; what furniture you currently have and what furniture you may need to buy (see pages 80–89).

ABOVE: A FLOOR-TO-CEILING CURVED WINDOW OFFERS A FABULOUS PANORAMIC VIEW. THE SEATING HAS THEREFORE BEEN POSITIONED TO MAKE THE MOST OF THE VANTAGE POINT.

OPPOSITE: WHERE SPACE IS LIMITED, CHOOSE FURNITURE THAT FITS EXACTLY. HERE, L-SHAPED SOFAS HAVE BEEN MADE TO MEASURE, LEAVING ROOM FOR THE COFFEE TABLE.

Storage, too, is a major consideration when planning the design aspects of your rooms (see pages 14–25). The more time and thought you invest at this stage, the more satisfied you'll be with the end result.

These details might seem prosaic, but they can make a huge difference to a room: put a radiator in the wrong place and it could affect the whole layout. Misplaced power and TV outlets could mean unsightly wires being secured along the baseboards halfway around the room or even over a doorway or fireplace. Put in the wall lights before deciding where you want the furniture and you could find they don't relate to any feature of the room. Buy a three-seater sofa and you might not be able to fit in another chair, but having planned properly, you may have been able to squeeze in a five-seater. These details make the difference between "design" and "make-do."

Planning checklist

• *List all the room's activities (see pages 14–16)*

• *Zone all the activities (see pages 18–25)*

• *Assess the architecture (see right)*

• *Consider the heating (see pages 30–32)*

• *Decide on the focal point (see pages 30–33)*

• *Decide on the positioning of any home entertainment (see page 33)*

• *Decide on the size and positioning of furniture (see pages 33–34)*

• *Decide on the number and position of electrical outlets (see page 44)*

• *Assess the storage (see pages 68–79)*

• *Decide on the positioning of wall and ceiling lights (see pages 36–49)*

Assess the architecture

First, take stock of what you have. Look at the architecture. Where are the doors and windows? Is there a fireplace? It's rare to move the fireplace due to the structural role of the chimney, so most people use this as the focal point.

The positions of the doors and windows have a key role. Although it's usual to plan around them, rehanging an internal door to open the other way, or even repositioning it can make a huge difference to the space. Moving windows, however, has an impact on the outside elevation and structure of the building, and so should be done only in consultation with an architect.

The order of building work

By working through the project in a logical order, you are less likely to make design mistakes and more likely to oversee a smoothly run job while saving money in the long run. Before the contractors arrive, draw up a plan indicating the position of every power outlet, light (be it recessed, wall, chandelier, or pendant), and radiator. If you don't mind the mess, mark these on the wall itself. Before the professionals arrive to begin work, clear the whole room.

Once the work starts, this is the most likely order of events:
• **Modification of any infrastructure,** such as moving any walls or doors
• **Initial electrical work,** including installing wires for outlets and light fixtures
• **Replastering** or drywall
• **Electrical finishing,** including installing lights, outlets, and switch covers
• **Carpentry,** including any built-in furniture
• **Radiators installed**
• **Old floors refurbished**
• **Fireplaces refurbished/fitted**
• **Hard flooring installed and finished,** except final coat of varnish
• **Room painted and wallpapered**
• **Final finish for wood floors**
• **Carpet installed**
• **Freestanding furniture put in position.**

1 THE ARCHITECTURAL STATEMENT OF THIS PLATE-GLASS WINDOW GIVES A NATURAL FOCUS TO THE WHOLE LAYOUT.

2 FIREPLACES—WHETHER THEY ARE TRADITIONAL OR MODERN—ARE USUALLY THE FOCUS OF THE ROOM.

3 L-SHAPED SEATING CAN ACCOMMODATE A SURPRISING NUMBER OF PEOPLE, EVEN IN SMALL SPACES.

4 ENSURE YOU PROVIDE ENOUGH OUTLETS TO SERVE ALL YOUR LIGHTING AND HOME ENTERTAINMENT NEEDS.

Consider the heating

Traditionally, the fireplace was the main source of heating, and, apart from providing the heating, this became symbolic of all that is appealing about hearth and home. For this reason, the fireplace is usually the focal point of the room. Radiators, on the other hand, are usually located for efficient heating, rather than for their looks. The location of both the fireplace and the radiators has an impact on how you lay out the room. Here are the visual priorities when planning the heating:

• **Restore, rather than replace original fireplaces** if you possibly can. The original will always add design integrity to the room.

• **Keep an open mind if you keep the original fireplace.** Don't be afraid to offset a traditional fireplace with sleek modern interior design if that is your style.

• **Design the fireplace first,** if you've decided to put in a new one. It will be the focal point of the room, so it has to take priority.

• **Choose pretty radiators,** and arrange them to make best use of space as their positioning will affect the layout of the furniture. Although the plumber or electrician will decide on the best size and position from a technical point of view, you may want to rethink the style for design reasons. For example, if you have little wall space to spare, rather than sacrificing it to a conventional radiator, you could choose a tall, thin one that looks gorgeous, takes up minimal space, yet emits the correct amount of heat.

1 A TV SCREEN HAS BEEN INCORPORATED INTO THIS BEAUTIFUL EARLY TWENTIETH-CENTURY STONE FIREPLACE, CREATING A FOCAL POINT THAT ENCOMPASSES BOTH TRADITIONAL AND MODERN LIVING.

2 AS THE TWENTIETH CENTURY PROGRESSED, FIREPLACES BECAME EVER SIMPLER.

3 ADOBE-STYLE FIREPLACES, LIKE THIS ONE, HAVE A SIMPLICITY THAT IS AT HOME IN MODERN INTERIORS.

Fireplace options

choice	what	where
	French fireplaces, with their flamboyant curves and deep mantel shelf are based on the Louis XV eighteenth-century styles. Usually made of marble.	Although not typically Federal, these most elegant of fireplaces work well in well-proportioned Federal houses.
	Georgian fireplaces were the European inspiration for Federal fireplaces. Based on Greek and Roman architecture, they feature reeded pilasters, acanthus leaves, and urns.	The perfect choice for a Federal-style house, their elegant proportions also work well in both contemporary yet classic-styled homes.
	Hole-in-the-wall fireplaces are inspired by modern design: pared-down and minimal.	Best in modern and contemporary houses of the twentieth and twenty-first centuries.
	Medieval stone fireplaces are based on fifteenth-century European architecture. The large open mantel is often made of sandstone.	The simple lines work remarkably well both in period and modern houses.

Don't be afraid to offset a traditional fireplace with sleek modern interior design if that is your style.

Where space is tight, consider installing a tall, slim radiator that looks gorgeous, uses minimal space, and yet pumps out plenty of heat.

Radiator options

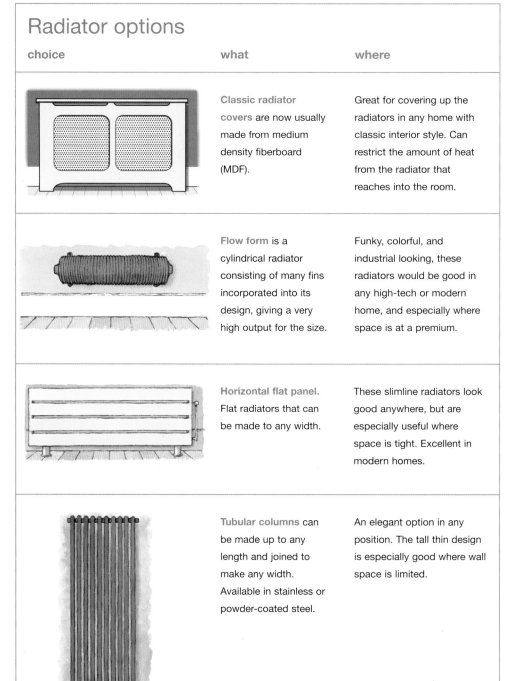

choice	what	where
Classic radiator covers are now usually made from medium density fiberboard (MDF).	Great for covering up the radiators in any home with classic interior style. Can restrict the amount of heat from the radiator that reaches into the room.	
Flow form is a cylindrical radiator consisting of many fins incorporated into its design, giving a very high output for the size.	Funky, colorful, and industrial looking, these radiators would be good in any high-tech or modern home, and especially where space is at a premium.	
Horizontal flat panel. Flat radiators that can be made to any width.	These slimline radiators look good anywhere, but are especially useful where space is tight. Excellent in modern homes.	
Tubular columns can be made up to any length and joined to make any width. Available in stainless or powder-coated steel.	An elegant option in any position. The tall thin design is especially good where wall space is limited.	

Position the furniture

Once the framework is in place for the living room, you'll need to decide where to position the television screen and/or sound system. This will, to a large extent, inform on the layout of the furniture as most of the seating should afford a comfortable view. With modern home theater arrangements, this may be more complicated as they can incorporate separate speakers for that surround-sound experience, some of which will need to be positioned behind the main seating.

The next priority is to work out how much seating is needed to accommodate at least the whole family. If the space is limited, this can amount to quite a puzzle; but it can be worked out if you draw everything on a plan. Make a scale drawing of the room and cut out the shape of each piece of furniture to the same scale. Arrange your templates on the plan to create your preferred arrangement.

THIS LIVING AREA HAS BEEN PLANNED FOR TV VIEWING AT ONE END WITH A MORE FORMAL AREA IN THE FOREGROUND. THE SOUND SYSTEM IS A PRIORITY OF THIS SECTION, SO HANDSOME DESIGNER SPEAKERS HAVE BECOME A FOCAL POINT, WITH SEATING POSITONED FOR EVERYONE TO GET MAXIMUM ENJOYMENT.

Be bold in your thinking. If your current furniture is no longer working for you, you may need to source other pieces. For example, exchanging a three-piece suite for two sofas could easily give you two extra seats and, if they are carefully arranged, at very little extra cost in terms of space.

Alternatively, you may completely re-think and invest in a roomy corner unit. Peversely, you can create a feeling of more space in a tiny living room if you invest in one or two generously sized sofas that almost fill the room, than if you furnish it with several smaller pieces. It's surprising how furniture can take up most of the floor space without making the room feel cramped, especially if it's providing plenty of seating. After all, people aim to sit down in the living room and there is little need for much circulation space, so long as each seat can be reached.

The other main living room requirement is storage space for all the various media, including books, DVDs, and CDs. There is a wide range of stacking systems and shelves available, that make best use of space while keeping everything standing up and orderly.

Once you are happy with the proposed layout of the room, you'll be ready to think about the positioning of the power outlets, radiators, and wall lights.

TWO GENEROUS THREE-SEATER SOFAS GIVE SUBSTANCE TO THE LAYOUT OF THIS LIVING AREA. WITH THE ADDITION OF AN ARMCHAIR AND OCCASIONAL CHAIR, THERE IS GENEROUS SEATING FOR EIGHT, YET THIS RELATIVELY SMALL SPACE DOES NOT FEEL CRAMPED.

lights

ABOVE: PLAN THE POSITIONS OF
WALL SCONCES EARLY SO WIRES
CAN BE RUN BEHIND WALLS PRIOR
TO PLASTERING.

OPPOSITE: RECESSED LIGHTS
HIGHLIGHT A PAINTING; OTHERS
WASH THE CURVED WALL.

Where lighting is part of the infrastructure, it needs to be thought through early on. Central ceiling roses are usually installed by the original builders, but if you'd like any kind of recessed or wall lights, these have to be put in before the decorators arrive. A hole will have to be cut into the ceiling for each ceiling light and installing wall lights will involve running the wires inside the wall, all of which are messy operations that should be completed before decorating.

Before deciding on the positions of the lights, you'll need to have a good idea of how you would like the room to be laid out. The key to good modern lighting is flexibility, which is not too difficult to achieve using recessed downlights.

The electrician will tell you how many lights you'll need for the area and this will depend on the output from each lamp. These could all be wired to the same switch, or you may prefer to wire different zones to different switches so you can alter the lighting depending on the occasion and the mood. For example, if you had an open-plan living-dining room, you would want to be able to dim the lights in the living zone when you are eating, and vice versa. You may also want to operate the same bank of lights from different parts of the room. For example, most people like to have all the lights operable from the door into the room so they can be switched on and off as you come in and out of the room; but it's also useful to have banks of switches near to where they are zoned.

The mood of any room depends on the success of the lighting, yet for most of us, lighting can be the most difficult element of home design to grasp. This section aims to unravel some of the mysteries of the hardware—general through decorative lighting (see pages 38–40), followed by a look at lighting for specific areas in greater detail (see pages 40–44).

TRACK-MOUNTED SPOTLIGHTS
OFFER MANY OF THE ADVANTAGES
OF RECESSED LIGHTING, BUT
WITHOUT THE NEED FOR
COMPLICATED WIRING OR MAKING
HOLES IN THE CEILING.

General lighting

This is the overall light in the room. At its simplest, it is a pendant hanging from a central ceiling fixture, but this offers little interest and no flexibility. It's much easier to produce a more agreeable ambience by combining several sources. Wall sconces and/or several table lamps have traditionally supplemented single-source pendants, but nowadays, recessed downlights are also a popular solution because they're neatly installed into the ceiling and so work with any architecture.

Most recessed downlights are low voltage and used in conjunction with a transformer. Calculating how many you need is a job best left to the electrician as this will depend on the spread of light emitted from each fixture, the height of the ceiling, the color of the interior, even the age of the residents, as a 50-year-old will need twice as much light as a 20-year-old. The best plan is to over-light the space and have the downlights wired to dimmer switches in groups for ultimate flexibility. Use the downlights for direct down light, or, if they swivel, they can be directed to "wash" the wall, creating a softer, more indirect light.

• **Direct light** comes straight from the source and quickly drops away. The most obvious example is a lamp without a shade.

• **Diffused light** has been softened and spread out by being shone through a translucent material, such as a lampshade.

• **Indirect light** comes from a direct source that has been bounced off another surface, such as the walls or ceiling, spreading it out to make an even, easy light. To avoid glare, the direct source usually has an opaque shade or baffle.

1 ELECTRIFIED WALL SCONCES RETAIN THE TRADITIONAL CHARM OF THE ORIGINAL CANDLE VERSIONS.

 2 THESE RECESSED SPOTS EMIT DIRECT DOWNLIGHT. OTHERS CAN BE AIMED AT WALLS FOR INDIRECT LIGHT.

3 STANDARD SPOTLIGHTS WITH SOLID METAL SHADES CREATE INTENSE DIRECT LIGHT THAT'S PERFECT FOR READING.

 4 CANDLELIGHT, SHINING THROUGH LANTERN GLASS, HAS A SOFT DIRECT LIGHT THAT IS SO GOOD FOR ROMANTIC DINING.

SQUARE RECESSED LIGHTS SET INTO THE CEILING ARE THE SOURCE OF GENERAL LIGHT IN THIS ROOM, ECHOING MAJOR DESIGN ELEMENTS.

Accent lighting

Create theatrical effects using spots as direct lights to highlight features, such as sculpture, paintings, houseplants, or to create moody pools of light. Spotlights are designed to emit different spreads of light: the narrower the beam, the sharper and brighter the light. This is key to success as the accent lighting needs to "fit" the object, while giving out at least three-times as much light as the general light.

Feature lighting

Architectural features, such as coves or shelves, can be highlighted, bringing focal interest to the room while adding to the overall lighting. This is often done using fluorescent strips, though now there's a new generation of rope lights made up of many tiny lights, specially cut to length by the manufacturer to fit the space. If they are fitted 10–14 inches below the ceiling or top of the cove, they can wash the surface for a pleasing indirect light.

Decorative lighting

Modern technology means that the fittings themselves can be almost invisible while emitting far more light than traditional lamps. But not everyone wants to live in so minimal an environment and they enjoy the decorative part a lamp plays in the interior design of the room while contributing to the light levels within the room. Central pendants, wall lights, standard lamps, or table lamps are generally chosen for the decorative, almost sculptural part they play in the interior design of the room.

Living room lighting

Recessed downlights are useful for general light. Make sure they are wired to switches at all entrances to the room so they can be switched on or off, whichever door you are using. Pendants, and especially chandeliers, make a decorative focus at ceiling height. These should be wired to their own separate switch so you can operate them independently.

Table lamps can also be used for general lighting, and they, too, can be wired so you can switch them on and off at the wall. Using dimmer switches in the living room is essential if you want to be able to control the mood of the room.

Spotlight options

choice	what	where
	Downlights are available with regular or wide-angle beams. Wide beams provide more general light. Narrow beams provide intense directional light sometimes used to highlight a focal point.	Installed into the ceiling void at intervals to be decided by the electrician, depending on the output.
	Eyeball or swivel spotlights can be directed to bounce off a wall, for example, which diffuses the light.	Could be used to wash a whole wall to create a softer, more diffused light than from the direct spots, while making a feature of that wall.
	Single spots, such as this glass cube, usually have a narrow beam designed to create intense directional light.	A modern way to highlight a focal point such as a sculpture.
	Triple ceiling spots are surface mounted using the existing ceiling rose. Can be directed outward for efficient general lighting.	Any room where you don't want to damage the ceiling by installing recessed lighting.
	Wire spotlights can be surface mounted, and so do not require patching walls or redecorating after installing.	Excellent for lighting voids, such as under high ceilings, but can be used in any modern situation.

Both table lamps and floor lamps offer decorative interest in the interior, while contributing to the light levels of the room.

Decorative light options

choice	what	where
	Art Nouveau table lamp Very pretty brass lamp with flower-inspired glass shade, typical of the early twentieth-century Art Nouveau/Beaux Arts period.	A delightful accessory that is best used on its own in the living room, rather than as one of a pair.
	Ceramic-based table lamp A classic table lamp that comes in many base shapes, ranging from round or oval to those that are tall and slender, based on antique Chinese ginger jars, such as this.	Elegant in any interior, be it period or contemporary. They look good in pairs on a console table, for example, or use one each on side tables on either side of the sofa.
	Drafting lamp is a classic from the early twentieth century. It can be angled into many positions, making it the ideal task lamp. This basic idea has been adapted to produce many updated alternatives.	The ideal task lamp in a sitting room. This one can be clamped onto a shelf or desk, but they are also available as table or floor lamps.
	Floor uplighter shines indirect light up to the ceiling. Provides visual interest in the room and has the flexibility of being able to be moved around.	This modern design demands a modern interior.

Wall lights can be a decorative touch, evoking the candle sconces that were the main light source before the introduction of electricity. These are best positioned at some architectural focal point, such as the fireplace or in relation to a major piece of furniture, such as the sofa or a large chest. Depending on the shade, the light they emit may be:
• **Diffused** (if the shade is translucent)
• **Direct** (generally downward)
• **or indirect** (upward).
Some wall sconces provide two or even all three types of light.

Picture lights, too, are wall lights and their positions will need to be decided at this early stage before decorating. If you really can't think about pictures while the room still looks like a building site, just let the electrician know the rough positioning so he can allow for wiring them in later. Where the decorations are spot lit, the walls will have to be patched and finished at the very end.

FOUR HUGE, MATCHING STANDARD LAMPS MAKE AN IMPORTANT VISUAL STATEMENT IN THIS LIVING ROOM, ADDING A SENSE OF HEIGHT TO THE INTERIOR.

Lights for display shelves Strip lighting fitted to the underside of the shelves and wired to an independent switch both contributes to the general ambience and provides a delightful focus.

Task lights For reading, writing, knitting, or embroidery, ensure you have a task lamp to provide high light levels on your work while retaining the general mood of the rest of the room. Work lamps are the archetypal example of this. They can be desk lamps, table lamps, or wall-mounted lamps.

Decorative lights Finally, you may like to add decorative table lamps or floor lamps to bring both sculptural and light interest in key parts of the room.

Electricity Now is the time to also consider the power, providing double outlets wherever you're likely to need table lamps. The home entertainment system is becoming ever more demanding in its power needs and you'll need at least four outlets near the television and at least another four near any sound system. This may sound like a lot, but at this stage it is much better to factor in spare outlets than regret it later. If you plan to have a home theater, think where the speakers will be. You will want to make sure there is an outlet that does not require trailing wires across doorways or any other circulation areas. And don't be tempted to run them under the carpet as they could become damaged and present a fire risk. It could well be that you can make use of one of the double outlets provided for a table lamp. If not, install extra outlets.

Dining room lighting and electricity

Pendants A pendant over the table is the perfect focal point and provides an intimate ambience as the background lighting can be switched off while you dine. You may love the pretty look of a chandelier, or you may prefer a more modern look. Whichever you choose, position it about 30 inches above the table and at least six inches in from the edges to produce the required light while keeping clear of the diners' heads. You might also want to consider including a pulley to raise and lower the fixture.

Task lighting You'll also need some kind of lighting in the serving area, which was traditionally provided by wall sconces. This still works well, whatever your style. Like living rooms, dining rooms benefit from zoned recessed lights and strip lighting in display shelving areas.

Electricity You will also need to consider the sound system, which may be linked with that in the living room. Discuss your specific needs with your supplier early on in the proceedings as the sound engineer will have to run the cables from room to room at the same time as the electrician.

1 THIS PENDANT IS MADE UP OF A GROUP OF SHADED LAMPS THAT DIRECT THE LIGHT DOWN OVER THE TABLE.

2 THE TRANSLUCENT CANOPY HANGING UNDERNEATH A TRIO OF LAMPS TRANSFORMS HARSHER DIRECT LIGHT INTO INDIRECT, WHICH IS SOFTER AND MORE DIFFUSE.

3 A NEAT, FIFTIES-STYLE SHADE DIRECTS THE LIGHT DOWNWARDS OVER THE TABLE. IT IS BUT ONE OF A VARIETY OF LIGHTING TYPES AVAILABLE IN THIS LIVING ROOM.

Pendant options

choice	what	where
	**Chandeliers** The name derives from the French for candle holder. Hung with crystals to intensify the available candlelight, they are now available in electrified versions.	Chandeliers add interest to high ceilings. Naturally at home in period buildings, they also look wonderful set against the plain simplicity of ultra-modern houses.
	**Deco-style** "upside-down" circular pendants were developed for lower ceilings. Often made from glass, this one is made in a water-lily form, a typical motif of the period.	A pendant that provides a ceiling focus in any modern room by bouncing the light off the ceiling. It produces a soft, indirect light.
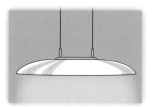	**Flat frosted pendant** with an elegant translucent glass shade provides a wide spread of light.	Clean, architectural lines make this the perfect solution for modern dining. Light diffuses through the shade and the downward light focuses on the table.
	**Flush ceiling lights**, such as this, are usually made up of a metal frame or clip with a close-fitting glass shade.	Perfect for modern homes with low ceilings, the glass shade creates a gentle and diffused light.
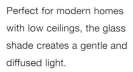	**Steel twist multipendant** A delightful modern solution made up of several low-voltage lamps for a spread of light.	This witty, feminine solution makes a decorative focal point over the dining table. The translucent shades diffuse the lights as they softly shine onto the table.

Wall light options

choice	what	where
	Art Nouveau brass light with flower-like glass shade typical of the period. The light diffuses through the shade and shines directly downward, creating a pool of light on the floor.	These can be used as a pretty decorative feature in a living or dining room.
	Candle shade-style wall sconce with updated modern styling. Candle shades throw some light upward to bounce off the ceiling (indirect) and some downward (direct).	Excellent for a contemporary home, adding decorative interest to the room and simultaneously increasing the general light levels.
	Carved wood sconce with two electrified candles. The intricate carving would work well in a period home, such as Federal.	Best used in pairs as a focus on a mantelpiece, for example.
	Modern glass with minimal styling, offering a combination of diffused light through the shade, indirect uplight and direct downlight.	A handsome feature to complement the architecture of modern homes.
	Uplight made of a paintable ceramic.	Excellent for any home to discreetly increase the light levels with subtle indirect light. They can be painted to further enhance the room's décor.

OPPOSITE: ADD DECORATIVE INTEREST. WALL SCONCES ARE TRADITIONALLY USED TO ADD INTEREST TO ARCHITECTURAL FEATURES. HERE, A FINE PAIR OF BRASS SCONCES PERFECTLY COMPLEMENT THE FIREPLACE OF AN ELEGANT FEDERAL INTERIOR.

ACTION POINTS: lighting design

1 CREATE A SETTING. A DRAMATIC PENDANT MAKES THE IDEAL LIGHT FOR DINING IN AN OPEN-PLAN LIVING SPACE AS IT CLEARLY DELINEATES THE EATING FROM THE SEATING AREA.

2 MAKE A VISUAL STATEMENT. HERE, A QUARTET OF ELEGANT GLASS TABLE LAMPS DO JUST THAT, SUPPLEMENTING GENERAL LIGHT FROM OVERHEAD RECESSED DOWNLIGHTS.

3 THE SMOOTH METAL LINES OF THIS PENDANT GIVE IT A CLEAN, MODERN FEEL, YET THE CANDLE-LIKE HOLDERS AND THEIR SHADES HAVE A TRADITIONAL CHARM THAT IS SUITABLE FOR MOST INTERIOR STYLES.

4 PLAN FOR FLEXIBLE LIGHTING. THIS PRETTY, WOOD-CARVED PENDANT AND THE WALL SCONCES ARE WIRED SEPARATELY SO THEY WORK INDEPENDENTLY OF EACH OTHER.

floors

ABOVE: THIS FINE ORIGINAL WOOD FLOOR IS MADE FROM HIGH GRADE, KNOT-FREE TIMBER. ITS SHEEN IS THE RESULT OF YEARS OF POLISHING.

OPPOSITE: FOR SOMETHING MORE HARDWEARING, HERRINGBONE-LAID BRICKS MAKE A DECORATIVE FLOOR THAT WITHSTANDS THE TEST OF TIME.

Of all the interior design decisions you'll ever make, the floor finish is likely to be the most permanent—so this is not a decision to be made in haste or too late in the planning sequence. Hard flooring, especially stone and ceramic, is almost part of the architecture and can be expected to last, or even outlast, the lifetime of the house.

It is sensible to play it safe even when opting for soft flooring, such as carpet or natural fiber flooring, as the cost and disruption of laying a new floor makes it unlikely that you will be eager to replace it in a hurry.

With interior fashions changing at an ever-increasing pace, it's easy to be swayed by current looks, but try to resist. Designers veer toward classic choices for floors as most color schemes team successfully with natural and neutral shades and so the floors will be able to cope with several changes of color on the walls as interior tastes change over the years. If you do want to add something of a contemporary accent, rugs can be the ideal solution, laid over either hard or soft floors. Large carpet squares, designed to take up most of the floor, can dominate the interior design of the room, so these should still be chosen judiciously. With smaller rugs you can have more fun, using brighter colors and more adventurous patterns.

Hard flooring is virtually a part of the architecture, so it should be chosen with permanence in mind.

Hard flooring choices

An exquisite hard floor that is in keeping with the architecture adds stature and integrity to the whole house. As well as great looks, hard floors are also extremely hardwearing and easy to keep clean—an important consideration for the ground level where a portion of the outdoors inevitably comes in. Whether you choose a stone or a ceramic or a timber floor can depend on where you live. In hotter climates, where preserving a cool interior rates high on the list of priorities, there are generally more stone and ceramic floors, while in cooler climes, wood is more often the preferred choice. However, they are not mutually exclusive—polished wood floors are popular in the Caribbean, for example, as much as flagstone floors are traditional in North European rural districts.

As a starting point, look at the local architecture, which often informs both the traditional and modern architecture of the region. The most usual traditional type of hard floors found in living rooms in your area is likely to be influenced by the available local materials. If there is a ready supply of local stone, that would have probably been the original choice of the settlers in that region, while a forested area would have offered a plentiful supply of timber. Even if modern transportation means we are less restricted in our choices, choosing a material that is traditional in your area will make your house relate more comfortably to its surroundings, making a subconscious link between the interior and the outdoors.

Stone and ceramic The most hardwearing floors of all, stone and ceramic have an air of permanence about them. Cool and easy to clean, they are most popular in hotter climates. In living rooms, where comfort and relaxation are the main function, stone and ceramic floors are often softened with rugs or room-sized carpets. If the living room is open to the dining room, an easy-to-sweep hard floor throughout makes the perfect choice, with the addition of a rug to soften the living area.

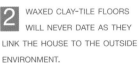

1 POLISHED MARBLE HAS BEEN A DESIRABLE FLOOR SINCE ROMAN TIMES, YET IT STILL LOOKS GOOD IN MODERN INTERIORS.

2 WAXED CLAY-TILE FLOORS WILL NEVER DATE AS THEY LINK THE HOUSE TO THE OUTSIDE ENVIRONMENT.

3 HARDWEARING TERRAZZO IS MADE OF MARBLE CHIPS EMBEDDED IN CONCRETE, WHICH IS THEN POLISHED TO A SHEEN.

4 STONE TILES ADD A GRAND APPEARANCE TO ANY INTERIOR. THIS PALE SHADE IS AN EASY-TO-LIVE-WITH FINISH.

Hard floors have been a popular choice for centuries, and continue to be popular due to their durability and lasting good looks.

Stone and ceramic floor options

choice	what	where
	Clay tiles and bricks Quarried clay that has been shaped and baked. Usually supplied unglazed, tiles are available in many shapes and, depending on local styles, can be waxed for a protective, shiny surface.	Locally made tiles or bricks have a rural feel that is more usually used in halls and kitchens. However, they can look wonderful in country cottages, softened with rugs.
	Glazed ceramics Clay tiles baked to provide a wide choice of colors, shapes, and sizes. Hardwearing, they can be used to imitate some of the softer stones, such as limestone.	Generally more suitable for warm climates, teamed with rugs for a softer, more relaxed feel in the living room.
	Granite An exquisite stone with a crystalline appearance that is available in many colors, from near cream to black. It is formed when molten rock under the earth's crust rises and solidifies beneath the surface.	Generally used in a similar way and in similar situations as marble. Offers a wider color range and with a more spotted look than marble.
	Limestone This fine-textured stone in sandy-gray tones is created under the pressure of layers of shells and sand. Not as hardwearing as granite or marble. Often quarried locally.	The cool, tactile feel of stone makes it an elegant choice. In colder climates, it is more likely to be used in utility rooms, such as halls and kitchens, than in living rooms.
	Marble A beautiful stone, often incorporating delicate veining. It can be polished to a high gloss and is very hardwearing, having been transformed from limestone by heat and pressure beneath the earth's surface.	Much sought-after since Roman times, marble is a sophisticated finish. Cool to the touch, it is popular in warmer climates, and rarely seen in living rooms of more northern latitudes.

Wooden floors A popular choice the world over, wood comes in colors ranging from almost white to almost black depending on the species of the tree. Choosing the timber (and therefore the shade of the floor) is very much a personal choice. Paler tones were popular toward the end of the last century, while by the beginning of the twenty-first, interior designers were beginning to favor darker woods. If in doubt, the wisest option is to choose a mid-tone classic, such as oak.

As well as the tone of the timber, the overall look is affected by the graining and protective finish. Hardwearing and easy-care modern varnishes mean that wooden floors are easy to keep clean and there is a range of finishes, from high gloss for an elegant classic look to semi-matte and matte for a more contemporary feel.

• **Polyurethane-based** is traditionally the most popular type of varnish. Solvent-based, these varnishes are hardwearing and dry to a clear, non-streaky finish.

• **Water-based finishes** are very much more environmentally friendly than polyurethane, but since they are basically latex paints without the pigment, can leave brush marks when dry. Brushes can be cleaned with water.

• **Two-part epoxy resins,** designed for commercial use, offer the most hardwearing varnishes. Available both as solvent-based and non-solvent-based, they require professional application.

• **Oil is a traditional finish** that penetrates and protects wood for a gloriously natural effect that is surprisingly contemporary.

When choosing a wooden floor, there are many elements to consider: as well as the timber, grade, stain, and finish, you'll need to decide on strip floor, planks, or parquet (see overleaf). Many suppliers may even supply the same timber in varying widths and grades, either pre-finished with a variety of stains and/or varnishes, or unfinished. They can also supply samples of flooring finished with varnishes that are applied after laying. Don't even attempt to select in the showroom. The flooring will look quite different at home, so take home some samples and leave them on site for a couple of days. Even the same timber with the same varnish can look quite different, depending on the widths of the planks and whether it is pre-finished or hand finished.

1 DARK-STAINED WOOD FLOORS HAVE A LUXURIOUS EBONY-LIKE FINISH—AND AT AN AFFORDABLE PRICE.

2 LONG, RANDOM-WIDTH BOARDS EVOKE QUALITY THAT BELONGS TO A BYGONE ERA AND IMPROVES WITH AGE.

3 TWO-TONED PARQUET CREATES AN UNUSUAL DIAMOND PATTERN ON THIS LIVING ROOM FLOOR.

Wood options

Ash The combination of handsome graining and pale good looks with resilience and flexibility adds up to an attractive, hardwearing flooring.

Bamboo Technically a grass, bamboo is becoming increasingly popular as a flooring with a cool contemporary look. Resilient and durable, it is also moisture resistant, and so is suitable even for below-ground living rooms.

Beech A fine-grained wood with a pale pinkish-brown tint. Very hardwearing, it is tough enough for the most used of domestic situations.

Birch The fine, dense texture of birch renders it as strong as oak. Found growing even in Polar regions, its natural waxes make it waterproof and extremely durable. The even, pale yellow brown and fawn tones make it a smart choice for floors.

Cherry An attractive rich, glowing wood with pink-red tones. Also available in golden yellows.

Oak Strong and durable with an attractive grain, this mid-toned timber has been a flooring favorite for hundreds of years.

Pine A popular softwood that is admired for its pale yellow tones and knotted, open grain. Not as hardwearing as the hardwoods, it was nevertheless the timber of choice in many period houses, and continues to be a perennial favorite.

Sycamore and maple These very hard, fine-grained woods are excellent for domestic use in high traffic areas, such as the living room. Often cream white, they are also available in darker browns.

Teak A deep red-brown timber from the tropics, teak is extremely hard and fine-grained. Although associated with rainforest logging, there are now many reputable suppliers who only offer tropical timber from sustainable sources.

YOU CAN CREATE VERY DIFFERENT LOOKS WITH THE SAME WOOD, DEPENDING ON THE WIDTH AND LENGTHS OF EACH FLOORBOARD AND THE STAINS AND THE VARNISH YOU USE. THIS BLACK-STAINED FLOOR PROVIDES A SUITABLY MODERN FINISH FOR THIS DINING ROOM.

Timber floor types

Acrylic impregnated floors Originally developed for commercial flooring that needed to be super hardwearing, the timber of these floors has been injected with acrylic for extra strength, making them perfect for all those hardworking areas.

Parquet Parquet flooring consists of small pieces laid to create attractive geometric patterns. This was traditionally done piece by piece by hand. Nowadays, it is more usually supplied as engineered blocks where the pieces have been laminated in a parquet design onto larger squares of plywood, making for quicker, easier laying.

Prefinished These floors are ready-finished straight from the factory and often more hardwearing than those that are finished after laying. Prefinishing reduces the time needed for installation. Finishes can be high gloss or semi-gloss polyurethane for a classic look, or wire-brushed or oiled for something that is more contemporary.

Solid boards Traditional solid wood floorboards may be tongue and grooved, which are invisibly nailed together if they are less than six inches wide. Wider than that, and they will also have to be screwed and plugged through the top. Even so, wider boards create an illusion of grandeur and look wonderful in well-proportioned rooms. Solid boards are not suitable for floors below ground level, or areas of high humidity.

Strip or engineered flooring These are strips of natural wood laminated onto a plywood base, resulting in a stable flooring that is less likely to warp than solid boards. Excellent for below-the-ground floors, or any high-humidity situation.

Timber grades and cuts

Rustic This grade shows all the knots, grades, variegations, wormholes, and general characteristics of the timber.

Second grade Showing plenty of variegation, most of the worst imperfections, such as the wormholes and largest knots, have been removed.

First grade This top-grade timber has natural color variations while being almost clear of knots.

Select High-quality flooring that is almost free of knots and other variations in the wood.

Clear This is the most expensive timber because it is virtually free of defects.

Plain sawn This timber has been sawn down the length of the trunk, making most use of the wood. The result is floorboards with plenty of variation since the grain varies depending on whether it was cut from the center of the log or nearer to the outside. It also expands and contracts differently according to where it was cut, so plain sawn boards are typically less stable than quarter sawn (see below).

Quarter sawn Here, the log has first been cut into quarters along its length and then cut into boards in a series of cuts perpendicular to the tree's rings. This makes for a more stable floor with an elegant overall look. However, as there is more waste, quarter sawn is usually pricier.

ACTION POINTS: hard flooring

1 CHOOSE HARD FLOORING IN NEUTRAL COLORS. THEY ARE LESS LIKELY TO DATE AND WILL BLEND IN WITH LATER INTERIOR DESIGN CHANGES. CERAMIC TILES LIKE THESE ARE OFTEN MADE TO MIMIC THE COLORS OF LOCAL LIMESTONE. HOWEVER, THEY ARE MORE DURABLE AND ARE LESS LIKELY TO STAIN.

2 FOR A COZY FEEL, USE DARKER COLORS. TO ENHANCE YOUR CHOICE, USE NATURAL WOODS AND EARTHY TONES ELSEWHERE IN THE ROOM.

3 USE PALE COLORS TO REFLECT LIGHT. LIMED OAK FLOORS ARE TYPICAL OF SWEDISH STYLE, BOUNCING DAYLIGHT AROUND THE ROOM. A SIMILAR LOOK CAN BE ACHIEVED USING A TINTED VARNISH.

4 STRIP WOOD FLOORING IS THE PERFECT FINISH FOR CONTEMPORARY STYLING. IT IS ALSO DURABLE AND VERY EASY TO KEEP CLEAN.

Soft flooring choices

For sheer comfort and luxury, nothing beats soft flooring. Easy underfoot, warm, and available in seemingly endless colors and textures, soft flooring also works as an excellent insulator, which is why it is popular in cooler climates. Soft floorings are also quicker and easier to install than hard, which means you can afford to indulge in a trendier look than if you're choosing a hard floor. Carpet is the classic soft floor, though the natural fibers, such as coir and jute, which were traditionally confined to providing the backing material, have now become handsome, hardwearing alternatives.

Carpet Glorious plain colors, intricate patterns, and fabulous textures all add up to a vast range of design choices, making carpet a popular living room solution. Traditionally, carpet squares or rugs were used on top of hard floors, and this has made a successful contemporary comeback because it combines the quality of a hard floor with fashion elements, such as color, texture, and pattern. However, wall-to-wall carpeting, an enduring product in the twentieth century for its seamless "background" against which the rest of the furnishings are set, has proved itself perennially popular. You'll need a hardwearing carpet to stand up to the rigors of daily use in the living room. Many carpets are made in several qualities, with the most hardwearing designed for halls and stairs, followed by living areas, and lastly bedrooms, which get less wear. Ensure you tell the supplier that you need living room quality.

Natural fiber flooring Hardwearing, textured, and contemporary looking, natural flooring is being installed in the most stylish of homes. Its appeal is the easy-to-live-with neutral tones that team with most color schemes, plus its natural resilience to staining. Although much easier to install than hard flooring, natural fiber flooring is neither as flexible nor as stable as conventional carpeting. Requiring a double adhesive method of installation, many carpet specialists are reluctant to lay natural fiber flooring, but it's worth the effort in terms of long-lived, timeless good looks.

1 WALL-TO-WALL VELVET CARPET INTRODUCES A SENSE OF LUXURY AND UNITY TO THE LIVING ROOM.

2 USE LOOPS AND TUFTS TO CREATE TEXTURAL PATTERN. THIS GEOMETRIC DESIGN IS APPEALINGLY FRESH AND MODERN.

3 SIMPLE GEOMETRICS, SUCH AS THIS, LOOK ESPECIALLY HANDSOME WHEN NEUTRAL COLORS ARE USED.

Carpet glossary

Axminster Quality traditional multicolored carpets are often made by the Axminster method, whereby the tufts are woven into the backing from above using a jacquard mechanism.

Berber Inspired by Saharan nomads, these carpets are made from heavy, natural-colored yarn and incorporate interesting chunky textures.

Bonded An economical method of making single-color carpets by bonding tufts onto a backing using a PVC compound.

Cut and loop Here, some of the tufts are cut, thereby creating various textures.

Density Dense carpets stand up well to wear and are less likely to flatten than those that are less dense. Test density by bending back the sample to check how closely the tufts are placed.

Hard twist A hardwearing cut pile created by using yarn that has been given a permanent twist.

Loop Continuous rows of uncut loops. The loops are sometimes all the same height, sometimes multi-level to create interesting textures. They are hardwearing.

Multiframe Wilton A multi-frame Wilton can combine a cut and loop pile to create textured effects as well as multicolored carpets. As the color not visible on the surface is carried inside the backing layer, this produces a dense, luxurious carpet that rarely consists of more than two or three colors.

Shag pile A long cut pile that feels luxurious. Ensure the pile is high density, or it will tend to flatten with wear.

Tufted Tufts are inserted into a backing, which is then coated with latex. A secondary backing adds depth and strength. This is a less expensive method than the Axminster or Wilton weave.

Velvet A cut pile carpet that has been woven using low-twist yarn for a classic, smooth look.

Wilton High-quality single-color carpets are likely to be woven by the Wilton method, where the backing and pile are woven at the same time from a single strand of yarn.

Carpet fibers

Acrylic The closest synthetic fiber to wool in appearance. However, it is more likely to flatten and show staining than its natural cousin.

Nylon or polyamide More resilient than wool, but more inclined to flatten and attract stains. Sometimes, the fibers are crimped to give the impression of a denser pile.

Polyester This is a soft fiber that gives a luxurious look to deeper pile carpets. It is inclined to flatten, however, so look for a dense pile if this is the fiber for you.

Polypropylene Hardwearing and inexpensive, polypropylene is often used mixed with other fibers.

Pure new wool The ultimate in luxury, wool has excellent body, can be dyed to glorious colors, is less likely to flatten than any other fiber and is naturally stain resistant. However, it is expensive, so is often mixed 80% wool, 20% synthetic fiber, which can also provide extra resilience.

Viscose An inexpensive synthetic fiber that is often used to bulk out other fibers.

Natural floor choices

Coir Made from the outer husk of coconut spun into yarn, this is the traditional fiber used for entrance matting. Woven into herringbone and basket weave designs, it provides a handsome and durable solution for heavy traffic areas.

Jute Traditionally used for making rope, jute is nevertheless the softest and most wool-like of the naturals. It is very durable.

Seagrass A pleasing, slubby fiber that makes for an attractive open weave. Low in absorbency, it is easy to maintain, though its slightly slippery surface makes it unsuitable for stairs.

Sisal A durable fiber made from a cactus-like, subtropical plant, which weaves into a closely woven material that is naturally antistatic and non-absorbent, making it an easy-care flooring.

NATURAL FIBERS, SUCH AS COIR, MAKE AN IDEAL FLOORING. THEIR NEUTRAL TONES ALWAYS COMBINE WELL WITH SUCCESSIVE CHANGES OF COLOR SCHEME. THEY ARE ALSO DURABLE, RESILIENT, AND STAIN RESISTANT. NATURAL FLOORINGS WORK WELL BOTH AS WALL-TO-WALL COVERINGS AND WITH THE EDGES BOUND AND LAID ON TOP OF A HARD FLOOR, AS SEEN HERE.

ACTION POINTS: soft and natural flooring

1 THE NATURAL TONES OF SISAL ARE PERFECT FOR EVEN THE MOST ELEGANT OF INTERIORS, AND THE MATERIAL'S DURABLE, STAIN-RESISTING QUALITIES KEEP IT THAT WAY.

2 JUTE IS THE MOST LUXURIOUS, WOOL-LIKE NATURAL FIBER. HERE, IT IS USED WALL TO WALL FOR A CONTEMPORARY FEEL, WHILE PROVIDING A COMMON LINK FOR THREE DIFFERENT ZONES WITHIN THE ROOM.

3 CONTRASTING WEFT AND WARP FIBERS CREATE A LOVELY GEOMETRIC PATTERN ON THIS LOOPED CARPET.

4 LOOP-WOVEN FLOORING OFFERS INTERESTING TEXTURE TO THE WHOLE INTERIOR. HERE, IT IS THE PERFECT LINK FOR AN ECLECTIC MIX OF MODERN AND TRADITIONAL FURNITURE.

ACTION POINTS: combining flooring types

1 ZONE AREAS. HERE, A SLEEK WOODEN FLOOR STRETCHES THROUGHOUT THE WHOLE APARTMENT. HOWEVER, IN THE SEATING AREA, IT IS OVERLAID BY A SUMPTUOUS DEEP PILE TWIST RUG THAT DEFINES THE AREA AND PROVIDES LUXURIOUS COMFORT.

2 COMBINE DIFFERENT TEXTURES. THIS LIVING ROOM FLOOR IS CLAD IN WOOD; ITS ADJACENT SPACE IS STONE, THEREBY DELINEATING THE DIFFERENT AREAS. THE CARPET SQUARE FURTHER "GROUNDS" THE SEATING AREA.

3 BE PREPARED TO CONTRAST COLORS. A WHITE CARPET STRIP EMPHASIZES THE CRISP WHITE FURNITURE IN THIS SEATING AREA. SET ON A DARK WOODEN FLOOR, THE COLOR VARIATION SHARPENS THE FINISHED EFFECT.

4 ADD WARMTH. CARPET GIVES EXTRA COMFORT TO HOMES IN NORTHERN CLIMES. WITH A HARD FLOOR, THE ROOM COULD FEEL CHILLY.

storage

ABOVE: THIS BEAUTIFUL ANTIQUE
SECRETARY MAKES ATTRACTIVE
LIVING ROOM STORAGE, WITH
BOOKSHELVES AND A GENEROUS
DRAWER FOR STATIONERY.

OPPOSITE: A PAIR OF PRETTY
BUILT-IN CABINETS AND A
CUPBOARD PROVIDE AMPLE
STORAGE IN THIS DINING ROOM.

Feng shui experts remind us that when there's a place for everything and everything is in its place, we can live in a space of clutter-free calm, which makes us feel so much better. But even if you're not one of those super-tidy people, there's no denying that well-thought-out storage is the key to an organized life. If you're redesigning any room, it's worth making this a priority. With space for everything, cleaning up becomes a breeze, and with everything neatly put away, you can keep the surfaces in the room clear and clutter free.

By planning the storage early on in the design process, you can ensure you allow for enough, while making the best possible use of space. You need to think of storage in terms of the overall interior design, assessing what space you have available to either build-in or position freestanding pieces. From a practical point of view, assess what you need to store and how it will be stowed away.

Assessing what storage you need is as much about the scale of the items as it is about the cubic footage it is likely to take up. Deep shelves, for example, provide plenty of volume, but that's no good if you need somewhere to store your CDs. You'll need narrower shelves, spaced to fit the size of the CDs.

Most of us can't get enough storage space, and so have to think laterally. Building-in makes best use of the space as every spare inch can be incorporated into useful storage. You can also use spare nooks and crannies. The obvious solutions, for example, are to use alcoves on either side of the fireplace for cabinets, shelving, or a combination of both. Or you could steal just nine inches all along one wall to provide shallow closets or shelves without making a huge difference to the room's dimensions.

A MODERN LACQUERED BUFFET
BRINGS STYLISH STORAGE TO THE
DINING ROOM. FREESTANDING, IT
IS EASILY MOVED WHEN IT COMES
TO CHANGING HOMES.

Freestanding or built-in?

Do you love everything sleek and wall-to-wall built-in? Or are you more of a freestanding furniture person? This needs to be addressed early on as built-in furniture needs to be completed before the room can be decorated.

Built-in furniture represents the most efficient use of space, utilizing areas that freestanding pieces can't touch. Custom-designed to fit, it can smooth over alcoves and niches, stretch from floor to ceiling, wall to wall, and make use of every spare square inch of space for ultimate efficiency. Even narrow cupboards, when fitted with shelves up to the ceiling, can provide a surprising amount of square footage in which you can store, stack, and stow away.

Built-in storage is popular with modern architects, but it is no modern invention. Colonial and Federal houses often had walls of paneled cupboards; the Shakers were well known for their efficient flat-fronted, floor-to-ceiling chests of drawers. And while they, in their way, disguised the storage as walls, modern architects have brought the idea to new dimensions, using handle-free, touch-to-open doors for a sleek, unembellished finish. If this is a touch minimalist for your personal tastes, choose open shelving or a modular system than combines cabinets with open cubby holes for display.

Freestanding storage furniture can look less regimented, adding more of a three-dimensional element to the room. It can also transcend time and place. You may have inherited some pieces your grandmother loved, that you remember taking up different corners in different homes throughout your life. Or you may have bought a piece of furniture yourself, simply because you liked it; it's ideal for what you need to store and it's worked in successive houses. Another reason for choosing freestanding furniture is that you may not be planning to live in your current home for long, and you'd rather not invest large sums of money in something you can't take with you.

But whichever you choose: freestanding or built-in, it will impact on the overall layout of the room. As well as the dimensions of the furniture itself, you'll need to consider the doors, if there are any. This is particularly important if space is limited. Open

1 THESE CLEVERLY BUILT-IN CABINETS ENHANCE THE FIREPLACE, WHILE ADDING TO THE ROOM'S OVERALL ARCHITECTURE.

2 GLASS-FRONTED BOOKCASES ALLOW YOU TO KEEP ALL YOUR FAVORITE THINGS BOTH DUST FREE AND ON DISPLAY.

3 IF SPACE IS TIGHT, LOOK UPWARD. HERE, BOOK SHELVES HAVE BEEN INSTALLED ABOVE THE SEATING AREA.

4 A FREESTANDING CABINET WITH BI-FOLD DOORS PROVIDES GENEROUS STORAGE IN A SMALL SPACE.

shelves provide the most cost-effective, space-effective solution. For any furniture with doors, you'll need to allow space for them to swing open. If there is not enough room, look for a piece (or have a built-in designed) with smaller, folding, or sliding doors, or pull-down rollers. Alternatively, stay with the open shelving and fit roller shades at the front for when you want to hide the clutter.

Living room storage

With the proliferation of modern technology, living room storage has taken on quite a different character. There was a time when all that was needed, apart from display storage, was the provision of bookshelves and magazine racks. Now, we also need to think about the TV screen, CDs, DVDs, and games players. Much of the modern media is thankfully smaller than the old LPs and videos, and the chances are that it will get even smaller with time. But whatever the latest technology, in essence, it needs to be "filed" for easy retrieval. The best way to do this is to build or buy furniture designed to suit its dimensions. That way, it's both neatly contained and makes the best use of space. Most people continue to add to book and music collections throughout their lives that, along with family photograph albums, record memories and emotions which are difficult to discard. Once the space is filled and these things start spilling out from their accommodation, it's difficult to ever get on top of the clutter, so make sure you factor in expansion space.

Display space is the other major living room storage element. Many people use glass-fronted cabinets or display shelves. An alternative is to choose furniture that combines both display and practical storage, such as a Welsh dresser, which consists of cupboards with doors topped by open shelving for display. There are modern equivalents plus a generation of modular furniture consisting of drawers, cabinets, open shelves, and cubby holes that can be put together to suit your needs.

When planning your storage requirements, it pays to think through the following pointers before going any further:

• **List all your needs,** including the dimensions of the items you need to store.

• **Assess the storage furniture you already have.** Is it up to the job? Is it in the right place? Does it allow for enough space to accommodate the rest of your furniture needs, most importantly the seating?

• **If it's tight, think vertically.** You may be surprised how much storage you can make out of "dead" space, such as above doors (where you could, for example, store old books and music that you're not going to need to refer to on a daily basis).

ABOVE: LOW-LEVEL CABINETS HAVE AMPLE STORAGE FOR GROWING MEDIA COLLECTIONS.

OPPOSITE: FREESTANDING ARMOIRES HAVE GREAT CHARM AND LOOK EQUALLY GOOD IN TRADITIONAL AND MODERN INTERIORS. USUALLY FITTED WITH SHELVES, THEY MAKE EXCELLENT BOOK AND MEDIA STORAGE.

ACTION POINTS: living room storage

1 THIS WALL-TO-WALL, FLOOR-TO-CEILING, BUILT-IN STORAGE UNIT INCORPORATING SHELVES AND CABINETRY IS THE MODERN EQUIVALENT OF THE TRADITIONAL SHAKER SOLUTION. IT MAKES USE OF EVERY SQUARE INCH OF SPACE, WHILE PROVIDING FEW CORNERS AND SURFACES TO COLLECT DUST.

2 PRETTY, TRADITIONAL, PANELED DOORS CONCEAL GENEROUS SHELVING FOR LIVING ROOM STORAGE. PAINTED WHITE, THEY MATCH THE WALLS, CONTRIBUTING TO A LIGHT, BRIGHT INTERIOR. IT'S A CLEVER STORAGE SOLUTION THAT WOULD SUIT ANY TRADITIONAL HOME.

3 STREAMLINED AND MODERN, THESE BUILT-IN SHELVES ARE IDEAL FOR BOTH BOOK STORAGE AND DISPLAY SPACE. THE RESULT IS A PERSONAL TOUCH FOR A SLEEK INTERIOR.

4 BLACK-PAINTED SHELVES MAKE A GRAPHIC STATEMENT, VISUALLY FRAMING THE BOOKS AND ITEMS THAT ARE ON DISPLAY.

Dining room storage

China, glass, linens, flatware, candles, and candlesticks … these are the things you need to store in the dining room. They're all gorgeous to look at, and so they can make practical yet pretty displays. Traditionally, china and glass was often displayed on open shelves or in glass-fronted cupboards, and it still looks good that way, providing an attractive visual focus to the room. Flatware and linens are more often stored in drawers. A large sideboard usually accommodates all the dining room needs, though built-in cabinets serve dining room storage just as well. Choose a cabinet where the shelves are one plate or one casserole deep so everything is visible when you open the doors.

THESE OPEN SHELVES ARE BEING USED FOR BOOKS AND DISPLAY. THEY'D BE EQUALLY EFFICIENT FOR STORING CHINA AND GLASS, WHICH IS NATURALLY DECORATIVE, AND THE TABLEWARE WOULD BE NEAR WHERE IT IS NEEDED.

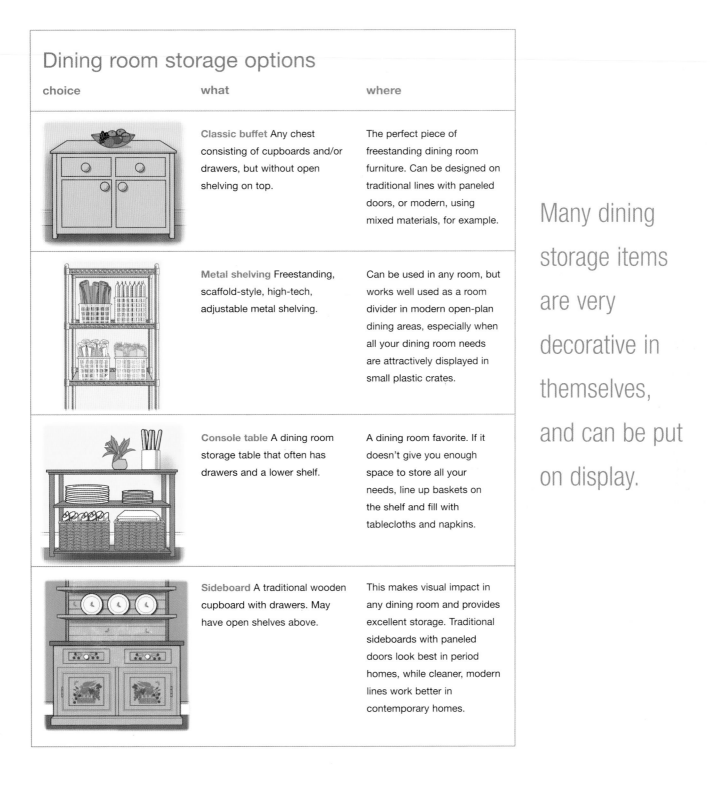

Dining room storage options

choice	what	where
Classic buffet Any chest consisting of cupboards and/or drawers, but without open shelving on top.	The perfect piece of freestanding dining room furniture. Can be designed on traditional lines with paneled doors, or modern, using mixed materials, for example.
Metal shelving Freestanding, scaffold-style, high-tech, adjustable metal shelving.	Can be used in any room, but works well used as a room divider in modern open-plan dining areas, especially when all your dining room needs are attractively displayed in small plastic crates.
Console table A dining room storage table that often has drawers and a lower shelf.	A dining room favorite. If it doesn't give you enough space to store all your needs, line up baskets on the shelf and fill with tablecloths and napkins.
Sideboard A traditional wooden cupboard with drawers. May have open shelves above.	This makes visual impact in any dining room and provides excellent storage. Traditional sideboards with paneled doors look best in period homes, while cleaner, modern lines work better in contemporary homes.

Many dining storage items are very decorative in themselves, and can be put on display.

ACTION POINTS: dining room storage

1 UTILIZE SPACE. IF YOU HAVE THE ROOM, INCLUDE A TRADITIONAL SIDEBOARD WITH DRAWERS FOR FLATWARE, NAPKINS, AND TABLEMATS, AND A CUPBOARD OR TWO FOR GLASSES. THEY ARE A PERENNIAL DINING ROOM FAVORITE.

2 MAKE A DESIGN STATEMENT. NOT ONLY IS THIS SIDEBOARD THE EPITOME OF CONTEMPORARY STYLE, IT HAS AMPLE STORAGE SPACE AND THE TOP IS THE PERFECT SURFACE FOR DISPLAY OR FOOD SERVICE.

3 USE COLOR. THESE PRETTY PAINTED PANELED DOORS BRING COLOR AND INTEREST TO THE WALLS, WHILE CONCEALING COPIOUS STORAGE FOR CHINA AND GLASS.

4 CHOOSE COMPLEMENTARY PIECES. THIS MODERN FREESTANDING CABINET PERFECTLY SETS OFF THE CHUNKY DINING SUITE.

furniture

When relaxation is the main raison d'être of a room, comfort has to be the priority for the furniture. This might seem obvious, but it can be surprising how uncomfortable some sofas are, while many dining chairs seem to be designed for a few moments of sitting, rather than for long, lingering meals. Apart from the design of the individual pieces, how they are arranged can also affect the comfort of the room.

When choosing both living and dining room furniture, buy with generosity in mind. Invest in the largest pieces that can possibly be accommodated in the room; once everyone is sitting down, there's very little need for circulation in either sitting or dining rooms. Generous furniture will be far more comfortable and give the space a more sumptuous look.

When it comes to sofas, large can, perversely, save space. A three-seater, for example, may simply leave "dead" space on either side that a four-seater may utilize while accommodating an extra person. By the same token, a single upholstered easy chair takes up a lot of space per sitter. Fewer, larger pieces will also make the room look far less cluttered than more smaller ones. Think in terms of pairs of sofas, corner sofas, and modular pieces that can make the best use of the space available.

Dining furniture can be much more flexible than sitting room pieces. Tables are often extendable and foldable to allow for easier everyday circulation, yet expand to offer seating for extra guests when entertaining. Many dining chairs are either stackable or foldable, or, failing that, spares can be used elsewhere around the house until they're needed for guests.

PLENTY OF PLUMP PILLOWS SCATTERED OVER LIVING ROOM UPHOLSTERY IMMEDIATELY MAKE THE ROOM LOOK INVITING.

EVEN LIVING ROOM FURNITURE CAN BE FLEXIBLE. THIS FOOT-STOOL CAN BE USED EITHER IN CONJUNCTION WITH THE CHAIR, OR AS AN EXTRA SEAT.

A COMBINATION OF SOFT FURNISHINGS, SUCH AS SOFAS AND EASY CHAIRS, PLUS OCCASIONAL SEATING IS THE BEST SOLUTION, BOTH FOR COMFORT AND VISUAL VARIETY.

Living room furniture

Although it's wonderful to have a large, light, airy living room, with careful design and clever planning, even small spaces can be made to look luxurious.

Scale Whether you go for larger pieces or delicate designs, the furniture must be of a similar scale. Even if a sofa is super comfortable, it will overwhelm the room if all your other pieces of furniture are much smaller. If you need a generously sized sofa in order to use the space most efficiently, choose one with longer legs that give it a lighter feel.

Color Re-upholstering is costly, so choose a shade that will not quickly bore you and will lend itself to several changes of color scheme. Either go for a neutral so you can easily change the colors around it, or choose a favorite vibrant color that you'll be happy to live with for several years to come, creating different schemes around it. Of course, even though three-piece suites were traditionally matching, upholstery can look equally striking if unmatched in coordinating colors.

Positioning Coffee tables look best if they relate in length to the sofa. How narrow or square depends on the size of the room and how it is arranged. For example, two sofas facing each other on either side of the fireplace would look better with a wider coffee table to balance the mantelpiece.

Upholstery options

choice	what	where
	Chaise longue A day lounger that is usually traditional in design, though there are a few modern equivalents, such as this.	Usually positioned as a focal point, such as in front of a window. A luxury in terms of the space it uses, so not usually seen in smaller living rooms.
	Modular units A choice of coordinating pieces designed to be configured to suit individual needs. Can include a regular sofa but more often have a corner piece, two-seater with one arm, and center piece.	Excellent in modern living rooms for maximum seating in minimum space. Can be arranged to stretch along two walls.
	Single chair Any single-seater upholstered piece. Often available with a matching footstool.	Traditionally, two were used in conjunction with a sofa (see below). Today, single chairs are often designer pieces used as a feature in the room.
	Sofa Available as two-, three- or four-seater. Often the key piece of upholstery.	Choose the largest sofa you can fit in the space. Traditionally, sofas were used in conjunction with two single chairs (the three-piece suite), to make for better conversation. They are more likely to be used as a pair facing each other in living rooms geared toward socializing rather than television watching.

ACTION POINTS: living room furniture

1 CONSIDER MULTI-SEAT FURNITURE. COMBINING PIECES SUCH AS SOFAS, BENCHES, AND CHAISES LONGUES WORKS BEST WHEN USED FACING EACH OTHER AS THEY MAKE FOR EASY CONVERSATION. OCCASIONAL CHAIRS OFFER A FLEXIBLE CHOICE OF EXTRA SEATS.

2 CREATE A FOCAL POINT. A GENEROUS COFFEE TABLE MAKES A GOOD FOCUS FOR THE MAIN SEATING AREA.

3 PLAN YOUR SEATING POSITIONS. FIREPLACES ARE THE NATURAL FOCUS FOR ANY ROOM, OFTEN BEING PLACED AT THE CENTER OF ONE WALL. USE THIS AS AN AXIS WHEN PLANNING THE FURNITURE LAYOUT.

4 BE EFFICIENT WITH SPACE. CHOOSE THE LONGEST SOFA THE WALL CAN ACCOMMODATE AND THEN SUPPLEMENT WITH CHAIRS SO THE WHOLE FAMILY CAN BE SEATED COMFORTABLY.

Dining room furniture

Living room furniture is usually arranged around the walls, but permanent dining furniture is more often centrally positioned in the room. Choose the largest dining table possible so there's plenty of room for everyone, allowing at least three feet between the edge of the table and the walls or any other furniture, such as sideboards, buffets, or consoles, to allow for pull-out space.

Chairs These need to be as comfortable as possible, to encourage long, relaxing dinners with friends and family. Traditionally, just the seats are upholstered, though fully upholstered chairs are not unusual. If the spill risk is just too high for comfort in your household, you might be happier having slipcovers made for the chairs, which can be whipped off and washed. Alternatively, you can choose chairs made of wood and make removable cushions for them, Swedish style.

Modern technology has spawned dining chairs in exciting new materials and combinations, so for a modern feel, choose from one of these. There are many plastics, including molded polypropylene, acrylic, and resin, plus combinations, such as leather and metal, aluminum and wood, wood and rattan, and cantilevered metal with woven plastic seats. Many are molded to body shape for extra comfort and have a wipe-clean surface.

Tables Modern tables, too, are often made up of combinations, such as metal frames with wooden tops, wooden frames with granite tops, or chrome frames with glass tops. The more translucent and light-reflective the furniture, the airier the interior will look, adding to the feeling of space.

Flexibility Dining furniture often needs to be flexible in its proportions, usually because there are limits on space, but not necessarily on the number of diners. It could also be because the dining room is transformed into a different sort of space at different times, or because there isn't space for a dining room at all. The simplest adaptation is a table with an extension leaf, or a gate-leg table, some of which have matching folding chairs. When it comes to chairs, there is now a wide choice in both those that fold down and those that neatly stack, ready to pull into place when visitors come to dine.

1 PAINTED WOODEN LADDERBACK CHAIRS ARE A DECORATIVE FEATURE IN THIS TRADITIONAL DINING ROOM.

2 GENEROUS CUSHIONS OFFER LUXURIOUS COMFORT IN A ROOM DESIGNED FOR RELAXED MEALS WITH FRIENDS AND FAMILY.

3 SIMPLE TRADITIONAL FRENCH-STYLE CHAIRS ADD AN ELEGANT, TIMELESS FEEL TO ANY DINING ROOM.

Dining room seating options

choice	what	where
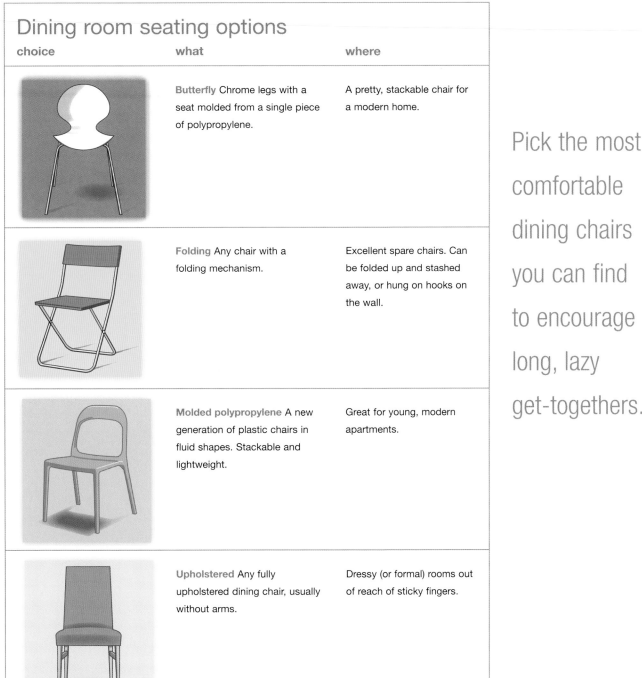	**Butterfly** Chrome legs with a seat molded from a single piece of polypropylene.	A pretty, stackable chair for a modern home.
	Folding Any chair with a folding mechanism.	Excellent spare chairs. Can be folded up and stashed away, or hung on hooks on the wall.
	Molded polypropylene A new generation of plastic chairs in fluid shapes. Stackable and lightweight.	Great for young, modern apartments.
	Upholstered Any fully upholstered dining chair, usually without arms.	Dressy (or formal) rooms out of reach of sticky fingers.

Pick the most comfortable dining chairs you can find to encourage long, lazy get-togethers.

ACTION POINTS: dining room furniture

1 USE SPACE CREATIVELY. NARROW REFECTORY TABLES MAKE GOOD USE OF SPACE AND CREATE AN INTIMATE AMBIENCE.

2 MIX AND MATCH CHAIRS. CHAIRS DO NOT NECESSARILY HAVE TO BE IDENTICAL. THE LONG BENCH-LIKE SOFA ON ONE SIDE HAS AN AIR OF ELEGANT PERMANENCE, WHILE THE DIRECTORS' CHAIRS BRING CONTEMPORARY APPEAL.

3 DECIDE WHETHER YOU WANT CASUAL OR FORMAL DINING. BENTWOOD CHAIRS GIVE CAFÉ STYLE TO THIS DINING AREA. THEIR NEAT DIMENSIONS ALLOW SEVERAL TO BE FITTED ALONG THE LENGTH OF THE REFECTORY TABLE.

4 THINK COMFORT. GENEROUS UPHOLSTERED CHAIRS ARE PERFECT FOR RELAXING MEALS.

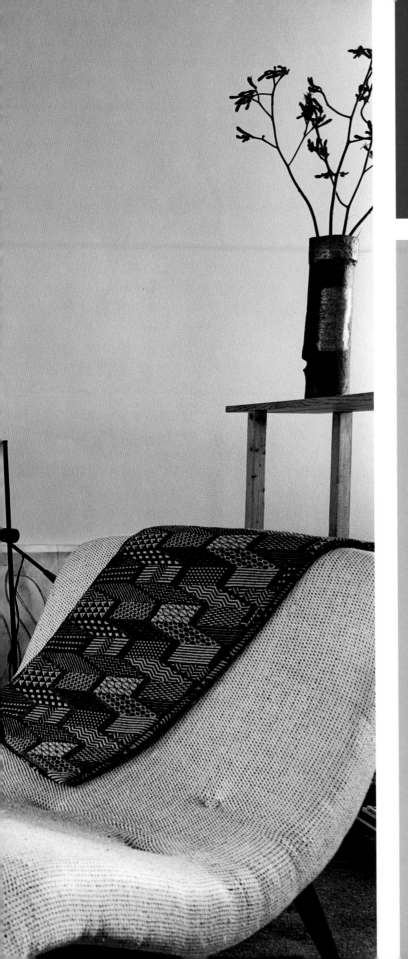

PART 2
decorate

decorative style

THE ELEGANT NEUTRAL SHADES OF
THIS CLASSIC DINING ROOM ARE
LIFTED BY TOUCHES OF ROBIN'S
EGG BLUE IN THE PAIR OF VASES
ON THE TABLE.

Good design is as much about addressing your lifestyle and making the room work for you as it is about style. It's about clear thinking and making sensible choices. Get the basic design right and it will endure fashion changes for many years. Decorating is the icing on the cake—the latest looks, the finishing touches, and the inspiration that gets you going.

Even if you are in the enviable position of simply needing to freshen-up the living room with a new coat of paint, try not to be tempted into a headlong rush of activity. It really is worth checking through the steps in the design section (see page 28) to ensure that you've looked at the space in terms of what you need before going through the expense and upheaval of redecorating. On the other hand, you may have just arrived at the decorating stage of a big redesign job, in which case, you might already have a file of inspiration and information. If not, now is the time to collect your ideas and research the stores for the fabrics, colors, and styles you like so you can start making up a decorating storyboard.

Color Whether you're going for complete redecoration, or simply want to update your interior with some fresh accessories, you will need to think about color. Even a few new pillows can bring fresh life to an existing color scheme. For example, you may already have pastel-colored sofas scattered with pastel pillows. Depending on the current interior fashion trends, you could update by adding a few neutral colors, or adding a few throw pillows in a richer shade.

Wall finishes If you are repainting or papering, think about the finishes as well as the colors. Do you prefer a flat or a gloss finish? Are you a plain-wall person, or do you prefer more adventurous effects? This is all addressed on pages 114–125.

Window treatments have a huge impact on the look of any room, so they need careful consideration (see pages 126–151). Not all treatments need to be expensive, especially if you choose panels hung at the windows using simple clips. However, once you get into lined and interlined drapes the costs escalate.

Finishing touches The final details, such as lamps, artwork, treasured memorabilia, or family photographs, are the personal touches that add personality, transforming

houses into homes. The way in which they are arranged and displayed can have as much impact on the overall look of the room as the items themselves (see pages 152–157).

From creating a color scheme to careful positioning of your favorite things, this section is packed with ideas designed both to inform and to inspire.

Decorating checklist

Whatever level of change you are planning, read through this list first to ensure you have covered all areas:

- **Look for color inspiration**
- **Choose wallpaper** options if relevant
- **Source fabric options** for drapes and/or upholstery
- **Choose paint color options**
- **Pin fabric and wallpaper samples** onto your storyboard
- **Buy sample fabrics** in short lengths
- **Buy paint sample jars** and apply to squares of card stock
- **Tack up fabric** and paint samples in the room
- **Once happy,** proceed with decorating/window treatments
- **Think about your finishing touches**

TOP: THE STRONG GRASS-GREEN TONES OF THIS SOFA MAKE A SHARP STATEMENT IN A CLEAN, WHITE-PAINTED ROOM. BRIGHTLY COLORED PILLOWS ADD ACCENTS.

ABOVE: PLUSH, CREAM THIRTIES-STYLE UPHOLSTERY LOOKS LUXURIOUS SET AGAINST TONES OF ELEGANT MOODY BLUES.

color confidence

The colors you choose for your home and the way in which you use them evoke the greatest emotional response. You can use color to create a feeling of calm, vibrancy, coziness, or relaxation. The idea that this can be done fairly inexpensively with a coat of paint can be seductive. However, with so many shades and tones to choose from, many of us worry about not getting it quite right, which is reasonable enough, given that differentiating between literally thousands of colors can be a challenge in itself.

Although everyone has his or her own instinctive sense of color, it can be further developed with the help of a little theory. Art students are familiar with the color wheel and use it to help them understand the subtleties of hues, tints, and tone by endlessly mixing different combinations. Without getting too bogged down in the complicated science of color, understanding the basics can help when it comes to putting together sophisticated schemes.

The color wheel is basically the colors of the rainbow arranged into a circle. It is divided into thirds by the three primary colors—red, blue, and yellow—with the secondary and tertiary colors between. Armed with a color wheel, it is much easier to understand color terms, such as color harmonizing and contrast. The difference between two colors can be infinitesimal, but the reaction you have to them can be huge. This could be due to the colors you choose to put next to them, it could be the ambient light, or it could be the expanse of the color.

A color primer

Primary colors Pure red, pure blue, and pure yellow, the hues from which all other colors are mixed.

Secondary colors Colors made up of two primary colors. These are violet (made up of blue and red); orange (made up of red and yellow); and green (made up of yellow and blue).

Tertiary colors Made up of a primary color and the secondary color next to it. So, for example, turquoise is made up of blue (a primary color) and green (a secondary color).

Warm colors Reds, oranges, and yellows are seen as warm, advancing colors that make a space seem cozy.

Cool colors Blues, greens, and turquoises are generally seen as cool and receding, adding a feeling of space to an interior.

Complementary colors Contrasting colors that are opposite each other on the color wheel, such as red and green.

Harmonizing colors Colors that are close to each other in the spectrum. So reds, oranges, and yellows harmonize.

Accent colors Used in small amounts, often in contrast to the main color. They bring the main color scheme to life.

Hue A color's identity. For example, as long as a color is discernable as blue, whether it is baby blue or navy blue, then its hue is blue. Black and white do not have any hue.

Shade A color that has had black added. You'd expect it to be muted or muddy.

Tint A color that has had white added, and includes the pastels, milky, and chalky colors.

Tone The lightness or darkness of a color.

When it comes to your own home, don't be afraid to work on your own emotional responses to color combinations. Be encouraged by the fact that there is no right or wrong answer: it's what appeals to you that's important. You also have an incredibly efficient tool to help you. The human eye can distinguish between seven million shades, so get your eye into training by looking at lots of different color schemes in books, magazines, houses, stores, and hotels. Start to note what appeals to you. Then, take your time putting the color scheme together for your room, following the steps below.

Find the inspiration. You may be inspired by a childhood memory, plants in the garden, the rolling landscape, the seaside, all of which may juxtapose shades you couldn't have imagined putting together. Alternatively, try flipping through the pages of books or interior design magazines. Store displays can inspire, too: you might spot gorgeous fabric that could be an excellent starting point for picking out shades to create a color scheme.

Match the colors. Paint manufacturers base their paint selection cards on the color wheel, placing the hues in spectrum order. Each card then presents that color in a range of tints or shades. This helps you choose, as you can start with basic color and decide how light or dark you'd like to go. It's a good idea to go one shade lighter than your initial choice as colors generally appear stronger over larger areas.

Try it out. It can be difficult to imagine what a color will look like on your wall because it will be affected both by the light and the size of the room. The best plan is to try before you buy. Have small sample jars mixed up and paint them onto foot-square pieces of heavy paper. Pin these onto the wall in the room both opposite the window and in a darker part of the room. Check them at different times of the day over a week or so to see how the changing light affects the colors. Only invest in room-sized quantities of paint once you are delighted.

Don't panic. As the first coat of paint goes on, you may have doubts. Most people do! It could be because there are still bits of old paint color on parts of the wall that affect the appearance of the new shade. It could also be that the color of a painted wall in an empty room can be overwhelming. However, once the room is furnished, this block of color will be broken up by the furnishings and fabrics. Try to see the job through—the chances are you'll be delighted by your original instincts.

Put it right. If, when the first coat has been applied, you really don't think you can live with it, you can always choose one shade lighter, softer, or even stronger to paint on as a second coat over the first. This should enable you to rescue the situation without too much waste.

Look for color inspiration, searching for combinations that you respond to on an emotional level.

OPPOSITE TOP: MIX BOTH COLOR AND THE FINISH—HERE, A FLAT NAVY BLUE ON THE WALL CONTRASTS WITH SUPER SHINY RED LACQUER ON THE CABINET—TO CREATE THE ULTIMATE IN A STRIKING BACKDROP.

OPPOSITE BOTTOM: DIFFERENT TONES OF BLUE ARE ALWAYS HAPPY TOGETHER, CREATING A LIGHT, BRIGHT SCHEME.

7 steps to color confidence

Monochrome schemes use different tones of the same color plus black or white for emphasis. This is a striking solution that's easy to get right.

Neutrals always look elegant. Ranging from off-white through string tones, creams, and stone to pebble tones and darkest slate, they look great in twos, threes, or teams of more. Use neutrals that are close in shade for a calm, harmonized scheme, or use plenty of contrast for a more exciting look.

Pastel shades, such as ice-cream colors, look great together. Mix the hues, but keep them to similar tones for a soft, feminine look that can also be reminiscent of the Adams style popularized during the Federal period.

Harmonize the hues for a restful look by choosing colors that are close to each other, such as blues and greens.

Contrast for impact either by using light and dark shades of the same hue or by using contrasting colors, such as black and white, red and green, or yellow and purple. However, as strong contrast does not make for a relaxing scheme, it can be more successful in living rooms to use contrasting colors as accents for a main harmonizing scheme. So, for example, if you have a mainly green scheme, you can intensify it with touches of red.

Earth tones always look good as they relate to nature and natural colors. Think terra-cotta, sienna, sand, burnt umber. Keep them warm and moody or lighten them up with some of the paler neutrals.

Historical colors, such as Shaker colors and those developed for period homes, take inspiration from tones that could only be made using natural pigments. The limited range, often with a velvety finish, makes choosing so much simpler. Easy-to-live-with muted shades that were typically used in Colonial and Federal homes still look stylish in even the most modern of houses.

ABOVE: NEUTRALS ALWAYS
HAVE A SENSE OF TIMELESS
SOPHISTICATION. THE ADDITION OF
BLACK BRINGS EXTRA DEFINITION.

LEFT: HERE, A BASICALLY NEUTRAL
SCHEME HAS BEEN GIVEN A
VIBRANT EDGE WITH THE
INTRODUCTION OF A LARGE
PAINTING, OCCASIONAL CHAIR,
AND SINGLE PILLOW IN
EXTROVERTED YELLOWS,
ORANGES, PURPLES, AND PINKS.

ACTION POINTS: creams and neutrals

1 CREAM ON CREAM IS A CLASSIC SUCCESS STORY THAT WORKS EVERY TIME. DON'T WORRY IF THE CREAMS DON'T MATCH EXACTLY: THAT CAN SIMPLY ADD DEPTH. HERE, POLISHED WOOD SIDE TABLES ADD DEFINITION TO AN OTHERWISE PALE SCHEME.

2 ADD ACCENTS. HERE, CITRUS GREEN ACCENTS PROVIDE A LIVELY MODERN EDGE TO TONES OF CHOCOLATE AND TAUPE.

3 BRONZES AND GOLDS BRING AN ELEGANT TOUCH TO MONOCHROME SCHEMES. THE KEY IS IN THEIR GENERALLY NEUTRAL, EASY-TO-LIVE-WITH TONES.

4 USE TEXTURAL CONTRASTS TO ADD INTEREST TO AN OTHERWISE MONOCHROME ROOM. HERE, THE CARPET AND CHAIR FABRIC ARE BOLDLY TEXTURAL AND COMBINE BEAUTIFULLY.

ACTION POINTS: hot and sunny tones

1 TONE DOWN THE BRIGHTEST YELLOWS WITH CHOCOLATE FOR AN ELEGANT COMBINATION THAT IS EASY TO LIVE WITH.

2 GIVE REIN TO YELLOW AT ITS MOST EXTROVERTED BY MIXING IN OTHER CITRUS TONES, SUCH AS LIME. THE DARK TABLES AND BLACK LAMPSHADE BRING DEPTH, WHILE THE COLOR CHOICES IN THE PAINTING ADD THE FINISHING TOUCH TO A SOPHISTICATED COMBINATION.

3 FOR A CLASSIC LOOK, TEAM SOFT BUTTERY TONES WITH POLISHED WOOD AND ANTIQUE FURNITURE, THEN LIGHTEN THE LOOK WITH CREAM.

4 THE HOTTEST ORANGE CAN BE DIFFICULT TO LIVE WITH. THE SOLUTION? TEAM IT WITH CHOCOLATEY TONES FOR A RICH, SULTRY LOOK.

ACTION POINTS: serene greens

1 THE COLOR OF NATURE, GREEN IN ALL ITS VERDANT SHADES IS EASY TO LIVE WITH. THESE SPRING GREENS HAVE AN UPLIFTING EFFECT ALL YEAR ROUND, TAKING A SOPHISTICATED TURN WHEN TEAMED WITH THE LIGHT AND DARK TONES OF CREAM AND BLACK.

2 SOFT, MUTED GREENS HAVE A LIGHT, CLASSIC LOOK THAT IS PERFECT FOR PERIOD HOMES. FUCHSIA-TONED DRAPES AND A VALANCE SET OFF THE GREENS WHILE ALSO ADDING A FUN, FLIRTY ELEMENT.

3 THE VIBRANT LEAF GREEN OF THIS FOCUS WALL WORKS WELL BECAUSE IT IS LIFTED BY THE ADJACENT YELLOW AND SOFTENED BY THE LIGHT OLIVE SOFA.

4 THE POINT AT WHICH GREEN IS VIRTUALLY YELLOW CAN BE QUITE A CHALLENGE TO LIVE WITH. HOWEVER, WITH THE SOFTENING EFFECT OF AMYTHEST, IT BECOMES ENLIVENING, YOUNG, AND FUN.

ACTION POINTS: blues

1 LIGHT SWEDISH BLUE IS ALWAYS A DELIGHT TO LIVE WITH AND WORKS WELL WITH THE PALEST CREAM. AVOID BRILLIANT WHITE AS THAT MAKES A MUCH HARSHER COMBINATION.

2 BRIGHT BLUES ARE WONDERFULLY CHEERFUL, ESPECIALLY WHEN OFFSET WITH OTHER COLORS TO ACCENTUATE THEIR INTENSITY. HERE, SAGE GREEN AND GENTLEST AMYTHEST ADD A SOFT, FEMININE FEEL.

3 TRADITIONAL LADDERBACK CHAIRS, PAINTED LAPIS LAZULI BLUE, BRING LIFE TO A FARMHOUSE REFECTORY TABLE.

4 CHALKY BLUE LOOKS LIVELY WHEN TEAMED WITH OTHER HUES IN THE SAME PALE TONES, AS SEEN HERE IN THE PINK AND GREEN DIAMONDS ON THE CHAIR.

ABOVE: ONE OF THE MOST
SUCCESSFUL WAYS TO MIX
PATTERNS IS TO TEAM FLORALS OR
FIGURATIVE DESIGNS WITH
GEOMETRICS. HERE, TOILE DE
JOUY UPHOLSTERY AND A STRIPED
RUG MAKE AN ELEGANT
COMBINATION.

OPPOSITE: VARYING THE SCALE IS
ANOTHER SUCCESSFUL WAY TO
MIX PATTERNS. HERE, THE SOFA IS
UPHOLSTERED IN HUGE BOLD
BLACK AND WHITE STRIPES, WHICH
ARE THEN SET OFF BY THE FINER,
MORE SUBTLE STRIPES ON THE
DRAPERIES BEHIND.

Pattern

Pattern can be more challenging to deal with than color, and, indeed, there are times when the use of lots of pattern goes out of fashion. But without any pattern, interiors can look very business-like and impersonal. If you're really not a pattern person, plan to introduce just enough to break the plain monotony. A tiny motif or neat check can make all the difference, providing subtle relief while retaining a restrained modern look. Patterned fabric has never completely disappeared from the decorating scene, but wallpaper has had a very quiet period. It is now seeing a renaissance, often in much bolder forms. While wallpapers were traditionally applied all over the wall, now it's quite acceptable to cover just one feature wall.

When choosing pattern for your interior:
• **Look at it in the way it will appear in the room.** So, if it's a fabric that will be gathered, gather up a section while still in the store, to see what sort of effect this has on the pattern. Some larger designs could simply become distorted in the gathers of draperies or pleats of shades, or a vertical design may be spoiled by the folds of Roman shades.

• **Look at it from the correct distance.** A small design might look very pretty close up, for example, but it might simply disappear when viewed from a distance. By the same token, a larger, bolder design might look great in a small sample, but be overwhelming when seen covering a whole wall.

7 steps to pattern perfection

Small motifs can have a subtle, almost textural effect, breaking up blocks of solid surfaces.

Go geometric with stripes, checks, trellis, or circles for a bold, modern look.

Florals are a perennial favorite. Choose one with a big bold design to make a statement.

Change the scale to mix the patterns. Where you'd like to team more than one pattern, let one be the leader, all big and bold, and complement it with something much smaller or one that is far less dense.

Be bold with a striking modern design set against strong plain colors, using fabric or wallpaper.

Mix geometrics with florals.

Animal skin designs are a timeless winner. They make a bold statement and imply a wild streak.

ABOVE: THE GEOMETRIC TEXTURE
ON THIS RUG IS THROWN INTO
RELIEF BY DAYLIGHT, ADDING AN
EXTRA ELEMENT TO THE INTERIOR.

OPPOSITE: TEXTURE IS THE KEY TO
THIS ALL-WHITE SCHEME. THE
WHITE-PAINTED BRICK CHIMNEY
AND DEEP-PILE TWIST RUG ARE
STRIKING IN THE WAY THEY
CONTRAST TEXTURALLY WITH THE
SMOOTH UPHOLSTERY AND GLASS-
LIKE PLEXIGLAS COFFEE TABLE.

Texture

Texture invites touch and adds to the sensory experience of the room. Who can resist running their hands through a furry pillow cover, curling their toes through a deep pile carpet, smoothing satin draperies? But it's more than that. Texture is pattern's sophisticated big brother, breaking the monotony of flat surfaces, yet avoiding the distraction of busy patterns. It is also architecture's best friend, and can be used to complement, and even accentuate the basic design of the room. Make a focus of a surface with a smooth, shiny material, such as mirror, glass, or leather, or add a deeply textural material like a chunky weave to a window, through which the light can create shadows for a dappled effect.

7 textural treats

Deep piles have a sense of luxury and comfort. Add a shag rug in the sitting room to invite kicking off your shoes and relaxing. A fluffy pillow would continue the theme.

Knubby loops add delightfully varied textural interest to an otherwise plain décor.

Shiny surfaces, such as a glass coffee table or wall mirror, add a sense of space and light.

Relief accentuates pattern. So, for example, light plays with an embroidered floral design in a different way from a printed one, giving it added importance. Add shiny sequins, and that brings even more attention to the piece.

Paler shades win when it comes to texture because the shadows more effectively accent the relief. Neutral schemes lifted by texture always look sophisticated.

Mix textures in a similar way to pattern. Contrast them for definition, rather than choosing two that are too similar.

ACTION POINTS: patterns and textures

1 BOLD MODERN CIRCLES IN BLUE AND TAUPE GIVE OUTGOING PERSONALITY TO THIS OTHERWISE UNDERSTATED DINING ROOM.

2 SMOOTH, PADDED LEATHER CHAIRS, CRISP SISAL FLOORING, AND A BRIGHT SHINY MIRROR BRING A SOPHISTICATED TEXTURAL MIX TO THIS MODERN, MAINLY WHITE, ROOM.

3 FLAMBOYANT FLORALS CAN SIT HAPPILY TOGETHER IF YOU MIX THE SCALES, AS HERE, WHERE OUTSIZED MOTIFS ON THE FLOOR ARE ECHOED BY SMALLER ONES ON THE UPHOLSTERY.

4 THE NEAT MOTIFS ON THIS WALLPAPER INTRODUCE SUBTLE PATTERN TO THIS CHIC, TRADITIONAL INTERIOR.

walls

In terms of surface area, the walls and ceilings take the major role in the interior. How you decorate them will have an impact on the whole look of the room, yet in terms of cost, they can be one of the least expensive elements. If the woodwork is in good condition, a couple of coats of latex won't set you back a huge amount, so this is where you can afford to bow to fashion influences. It's not so easy with wall coverings, however, which tend to be both more expensive and more time-consuming to put up. Steaming them off can also be a big job when you feel it's time for a change.

Paint offers thousands of glorious colors that have the potential to brighten your life. If your living or dining room has become tired or lackluster, there's nothing like a new coat of paint to bring it back to life. Also, there are so many ways you can use paint to create a different effect, whether you're trying to create an illusion of more space, improve the perceived proportions of the room, or simply update the room with the latest shades.

Traditionally, whatever color the walls are painted, the woodwork and ceiling are kept white or off-white. This both sets off the color, and, with a pale ceiling, creates an illusion of added height. Paint ranges based on traditional natural pigments often offer a seemingly endless choice of whites, some of which look alarmingly gray. However, your choice of "white" can be key to the overall look of the room. When choosing, try teaming the colored paint chip with several different "whites," then buy one or two test jars so you can try out all the combinations in the room (see page 97). Don't feel that you have to limit yourself to only using whites for the woodwork and ceiling. In Georgian times, it was not at all unusual to see the whole room, even paneling, painted in one color. This gives a harmonious overall look, especially if you are using quite a deep tone.

But there's no reason why you should keep to just one paint color if you don't wish to. Consider these ideas:

• **One wall of vibrant color** can look very striking in a mainly white room, especially if it's used to emphasize the architecture.

• **Create dramatic geometric Mondrian effects** using masking tape to make sharp edges for squares, lines, or stripes in contrasting colors.

• **Use two colors of slightly different tones** to visually improve the room's proportions, bearing in mind that paler tones seem to recede, making the wall appear further away, and darker ones seem to advance, making it seem closer. So, to make a long, narrow room look more square, paint the long walls in a lighter shade.

• **Hand paint a mural** (if you have the artistic skills), or try a subtle marbled effect. For those of us who aren't so confident, apply a pattern using stamps or stencils.

• **Look into the wide choice of specialty paints** that is available. They can be used to create metallic, pearlized, or translucent effects. Use these on whole walls, or in combinations with other paints. For example, you could create a checkered effect using different finishes in similar tones.

BELOW LEFT: SUGAR PINK WALLS GIVE A CONFIDENT IDENTITY TO THIS ROOM. YOU COULD CHOOSE TO PAINT THE WHOLE ROOM IN PINK OR, FOR A MORE MODERN LOOK, SIMPLY PAINT ONE FOCUS WALL WITH THE REST IN WHITE.

BELOW RIGHT: PALE LATEX IS STILL THE MOST POPULAR CHOICE FOR WALLS, OFFERING ULTIMATE FLEXIBILITY FOR THE REST OF THE INTERIOR DESIGN.

Paint options

Gloss/eggshell is a hardwearing paint designed for interior and exterior woodwork and metalwork. Traditionally oil-based, these are now made in water-based latex, which is more environmentally friendly and easier to clean up.

Latex is the modern, synthetic, water-based paint most usually used for painting walls and ceilings. It comes in flat, semi-gloss, and gloss finishes. Most manufacturers supply a small range of popular ready-mixed colors and a much larger range of colors that can be mixed up to order. Many can also computer-match any color from a piece of fabric or other reference. Smaller specialty suppliers offer heritage ranges based on natural pigments, which results in a much softer, velvety matte finish.

One-coat Available in a flat or gloss finish, this needs no undercoat, and will cover in a single layer.

Primers are designed to seal bare wood, metal, and plaster and prepare the surface for the paint to adhere to.

Special effects paints were developed to meet the needs of those who wanted an individual look without the bother of glazes and special brushes. They include pearlized and metallic paints, along with translucent washes.

Transparent glaze This thick glaze is used to create special effects, such as marbling, ragging, dragging, and stipling. It can be mixed with watered-down topcoats so other layers show through and/or used over the top of the final coat for protection.

Undercoat This prepares the surface so the topcoats adhere better, while providing excellent opacity that covers up previous colors so the topcoat will be true to the swatch color.

Varnishes can be oil- or acrylic-based and provide a translucent finish designed to show off the natural beauty of wood. Marine varnish is the most hardwearing.

ENDLESS PAINT COLORS CAN BE MIXED IN ALL FINISHES. HERE, THE FLAT AND GLOSS PAINTS HAVE BEEN MIXED TO MATCH SO THE CORNICE CAN BE PAINTED THE SAME SHADE AS THE WALLS. THIS HELPS MAKE THE CEILING APPEAR HIGHER THAN IT ACTUALLY IS.

ACTION POINTS: using paint

1 PAINT NEED NOT NECESSARILY BE APPLIED TO WALLS. USE IT ON THE CEILING, TOO. THE BOLD EGG YELLOW USED ON THE CEILING OF THIS LIVING ROOM GIVES THE EFFECT OF LOWERING THE CEILING. NOTICE, TOO, HOW IT REFLECTS OFF THE WHITE WOODWORK, BATHING THE WHOLE ROOM IN A SUNNY SHEEN.

2 A SINGLE COLORED WALL IN AN OTHERWISE WHITE SPACE CREATES A FRESH, MODERN LOOK AND SIMULTANEOUSLY ADDS A SENSE OF DEPTH AND DIMENSION.

3 GRAY TONES CAN BE SURPRISINGLY LIGHT-REFLECTIVE, ALLOWING YOU TO USE A MUCH STRONGER SHADE THAN YOU MIGHT EXPECT. UNDERSTATED AND ELEGANT, THESE SHADES OF GRAY MAKE A RELAXING COMBINATION.

4 THIS STRONG ORANGE IS SET OFF AND INTENSIFIED BY THE WHITE OF THE REST OF THE ROOM. THIS INTERIOR TRICK SPELLS CONFIDENCE, AND IS OFTEN USED TO BRING FOCUS TO ONE PART OF THE ROOM, OR TO AN ESPECIALLY NOTEWORTHY ARCHITECTURAL FEATURE.

ABOVE: STRIPES HAVE BEEN A
PERENNIAL FAVORITE FOR WALLS
SINCE FEDERAL TIMES. THEY WORK
WELL IN ALMOST ANY STYLE OF
INTERIOR, FROM CITY-SMART TO
COUNTRY CLASSIC.

OPPOSITE: CONTEMPORARY WALL
COVERINGS HAVE INTRODUCED
SOPHISTICATED METALLIC OPTIONS
THAT LOOK AS IF THEY'VE BEEN
PAINTED ONTO THE WALLS.

Wall coverings

For pattern, texture, and even foolproof paint effects, not much can improve on wall coverings. They take the guessing out of decorating because if you're in any doubt about your final choice, you can always buy a single roll and drape it against the wall in your room. There's a huge range available, from traditional florals, stripes, trellis designs, and even whole hunting scenes, to ultra-modern, dramatic designs. You'll even find a choice of ready-to-hang paint effects, such as marbeling, colorwashing, dragging, and stippling, which takes the guesswork out of how, for example, sand will look colorwashed over terra-cotta. Wall coverings can also add texture to walls. Some patterned ones incorporate a texture within the paper, while others, with embossed relief patterns, are designed to be painted over. Finally, there have been fashions for textile wall coverings, such as burlap, which is intrinsically textured.

Digital imaging has made a whole new generation of wall coverings possible. Images can be reproduced by specialty manufacturers to create custom-made wallpapers. So, you could, for example, digitally photograph a landscape, a flower, some bamboos, then have them enlarged to any size and reproduced onto a run of wallpaper. It can look stunning as a feature wall in an otherwise plain painted room.

Wall covering options

Digital imaging by specialty firms means that any image can be enlarged to any size.

Fabrics put up on the walls using a system of plastic battens give a very luxurious look.

Lining paper is used to prepare the wall for the main paper. It should be hung horizontally.

Paintable textured wall coverings made from linseed oil and flax fused onto paper are extremely durable and designed to be painted over. They are traditionally used for hard-wear areas.

Paper-backed textiles, such as burlap and flock, which is patterned with tiny carpet-like tufts, were very popular toward the late twentieth century.

Wallpaper is the traditional wall covering, and still the most popular. Available in a range of weights: the heavier duty the paper, the better the quality.

Washable and wipeable paper has been pvc-coated during the manufacturing process. It's a family favorite because sticky fingerprints can be quickly wiped off.

RIGHT: PANELING, ESPECIALLY
WHEN PAINTED WHITE, HAS
ELEGANT CHARM. NEVERTHELESS,
THIS GRAND LOOK IS BEST KEPT
TO ORIGINAL COLONIAL, FEDERAL,
OR OTHER PERIOD HOUSES WITH
HIGH CEILINGS.

OPPOSITE: THE SIMPLE TONGUE-
AND-GROOVE PANELING IN THIS
LIVING ROOM GIVES A RELAXED
SUMMERHOUSE FEEL TO THIS
PARTICULAR INTERIOR.

Wood paneling

Wood-paneled walls are seen more often in traditional than in contemporary homes.
In Colonial times, wood was an inexpensive resource, making it an excellent, readily
available wall surface. Not only did it very quickly transform the rough builders' finish
into one that was ready to decorate, it also provided excellent insulation. It is most
often waxed or varnished to show off the natural beauty of the wood. During the same
era in Sweden, wood-paneled walls were more often painted, making a lighter,
brighter interior, a priority in a land where winter nights are long and dark. This is
a style still emulated in classic Swedish style. An alterative wood-paneled style is
tongue and groove, which became popular during the early part of the twentieth
century with the Arts and Crafts movement. It had a revival toward the latter half of
the twentieth century.

ACTION POINTS: wall coverings

1 WONDERFUL CHINESE-INSPIRED MAGNOLIA TREES LOOK AS IF THEY HAVE BEEN PAINTED ONTO THESE WALLS. AS WALLPAPER, THEY ARE MUCH QUICKER AND CHEAPER TO APPLY.

2 THE ORIGINAL OF THIS WONDERFUL ALLOVER BLUE DESIGN MAY WELL HAVE BEEN HAND PRINTED, BUT TECHNOLOGY HAS BEEN DEVELOPED TO CREATE THE SAME EFFECT WITH MACHINERY.

3 WHITE-PAINTED PANELED WALLS HAVE A LIGHT FEEL THAT WORKS WELL IN BOTH TRADITIONAL AND MODERN HOMES. THOUGH DURABLE, THEY ARE NOT AN INEXPENSIVE OPTION.

4 WOOD PANELLING IS VERY OFTEN STAINED. HOWEVER, PAINTING IT, AS HERE, OFFERS MANY MORE OPTIONS AS YOU CAN THEN CHANGE THE COLOR OVER THE YEARS.

window treatments

ABOVE: SIMPLE PINCH-PLEATED
DRAPERIES HUNG ON A ROD BY
RINGS, IS A DELIGHTFUL, NON-
FUSSY SOLUTION.

OPPOSITE: ELABORATELY DRAPED
WINDOW TREATMENTS HARK BACK
TO THE EIGHTEENTH CENTURY
WHEN THEY PERFORMED A
DOUBLE PURPOSE: TO CREATE AN
ELEGANT INTERIOR AND TO KEEP
OUT THE COLD.

Windows are central to the interior design of the living room. Large or small, plate glass or many-paned, they can be adorned with glorious draperies or set off by simple shades. These are quite different looks, and how you dress the windows can be the key to your interior design preferences.

If you're a lover of draperies, you probably like interiors that are classic, comfortable, period, or romantic. Should you be more inclined toward shades, panels, and shutters, you're more likely to prefer a sleek architectural look. This can help inform your choice of furnishings. Having said that, neither has to be mutually exclusive—as a drapery-lover, you may well choose Austrian shades, which are equally sumptuous, but, being set within the woodwork are able to set off elegant window architecture.

By the same token, you may like a sleeker style, yet consider structured shades a little hard for the living room. A compromise could be delicate panels that bring a textile element into the room without the distraction of elaborate draperies. Whether you choose draperies or shades may also depend on the windows in the room. Being the source of natural light, windows play a key role in the architecture. This is especially evident in Federal houses, which were designed on classical lines harking back to the ancient Greek and Roman empires. However, not all windows have the best proportions for reasons that could range from the original design to recent adaptations. If that's your challenge, even if you prefer the sleek look, you may decide on draperies as these can be used to visually improve their proportions.

RIGHT: UNPRETENTIOUS CREAM DRAPERIES LINED IN GREEN GINGHAM EVOKE A DELIGHTFUL SWEDISH FEEL. IT'S A TIMELESS LOOK THAT TRANSCENDS FASHION AND WILL LOOK GOOD THROUGH SEVERAL RE-DECORATIONS.

OPPOSITE: VALANCES GIVE A CLEAN FINISH TO THE TOPS OF DRAPERIES. THEY CAN BE TAILORED, LIKE THIS, OR GATHERED AS IF THEY WERE THE ACTUAL DRAPERY HEADING.

Draperies

Traditionally, the design of the living room draperies is where textiles come into their own. Full and lavish, the most luxurious don't skimp on fabric, using at least double the width of the rod for generous folds and pleats. They're also lined and interlined, providing excellent insulation against winter drafts. Originally, most draperies were pencil pleated and hung on metal tracks disguised by a valance, cornice, or elaborate swag. Today, metal or wooden curtain rods with a choice of elegant finials offer an alternative to hidden tracks, bringing an architectural element to the overall window treatment. For an effect of further importance, add matching metal holdbacks.

BLUE AND GREEN WINDOW DRAPERIES HAVE BEEN MATCHED HERE WITH THE HANGINGS OVER THE DAY BED, GIVING THEM GREATER IMPORTANCE WITHIN THE ROOM.

• **Start with the fabric.** Since draperies don't get the wear and tear that upholstery does, almost any material will do, depending on the style of your room. Rich draperies in elegant silks, velvets, or brocades work well in elegant homes, while printed or woven cotton or linen fabrics work well in less formal interiors.

• **Check out the way it falls.** Test it by gathering up a handful. Look, too, at the effect on the pattern. Geometric designs, especially, can be "lost" on gathering.

• **Take home your favorite designs.** Hurried decisions can mean expensive mistakes, so before buying, invest in a half-yard piece to take home and look at in place. Gather it up and hang at the window to see how the light falls on the fabric and to assess how the scale of the pattern works within the room.

• **Decide on the heading style** as well as whether or not you'll want to have a matching cornice, valance, or swags, and/or matching tiebacks; all this will have a bearing on how much you buy.

• **Decide on a hidden track or a decorative rod.** Then choose one that extends six inches on either side of the window, if you have the space. To maximize the amount of light that comes through, choose one that is even longer so the draperies can clear the glass when fully drawn back. Allow at least an extra six inches for the finials.

• **Position the track or rod.** Six inches above the top of the frame is the most usual place for this, but to make the windows appear taller, you may want to position the track or rod higher up.

Working out the yardage

1 **Measure** the length of the rod.
2 **Multiply** by the fabric requirement for your chosen heading.
3 **Divide** this figure by the fabric width to work out how many drops you need.
4 **Measure** from the top of the pole to the finished hem length, then add six inches for hems.
5 **Multiply** the length (Step 4) by the number of drops (Step 3) for the final yardage.
6 **Always** ask the store to check your arithmetic, partly because mistakes can be expensive, but also because, depending on the fabric design, you may need extra to accommodate the repeat.

1 THE TOPS OF THESE SILK DRAPERIES HAVE BEEN SIMPLY TURNED OVER TO CREATE A SOFTER HEADING.

2 BY HANGING THE DRAPERIES HIGH ABOVE THE WINDOWS, THEIR SEMI-CIRCULAR TOPS CAN BE FULLY APPRECIATED.

3 BLUE DRAPERIES RUNNING THE FULL LENGTH OF A WALL ADD A SPLASH OF COLOR TO AN OTHERWISE NEUTRAL ROOM.

Traditional heading options

choice	description	fabric requirement
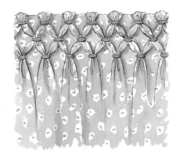	**Diamond smocked** These pretty draperies have hand-smocked headings, and can look delightful in cottagey interiors. They're best on smaller windows so the detail can be seen.	Twice the length of the rod.
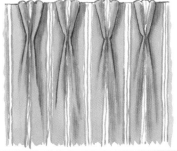	**French or pinch pleats** An elegant heading where the pleats are regularly arranged in groups of threes with a larger space between them.	Two-and-a-half-times the length of the rod.
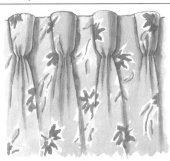	**Goblet pleats** A soft, feminine version of French pleats where each section is gathered, rather than pleated. The "goblets" can be stuffed with lightweight fabric to give them greater shape and body.	Two-and-a-half-times the length of the rod.
	**Pencil pleats** The classic pleated heading and the usual choice behind a valance or cornice. Pencil pleats also be used in conjunction with a curtain rod and rings.	Twice the length of the rod.

Tapes, tracks, and hooks

These are the secret ingredients behind the successful hanging of traditional draperies. Small and discreet, the tracks, tapes, and hooks work as a team to dramatic effect. There's a heading tape for most kinds of pleat, so all you have to do is sew on the tape and pull up the gathering cords for easy and effective results.

Heading tape options

French or pinch pleat tape comes in medium to deep widths with cords that automatically gather it up into groups of three pleats. An elegant finish that works well with taller windows.

Pencil pleat tape is available in widths ranging from two inches to six and pulls up into smart, regular pleats. The heading of choice when draperies are teamed with a valance, cornice, or swags.

Standard tape is about half an inch wide and comes with two gather cords. Perfect for lightweight draperies or sheers.

OPPOSITE: PENCIL PLEAT DRAPERIES ARE HELD IN POSITION WITH DECORATIVE HOOKS ON FINE METAL RODS.

BELOW LEFT: FRENCH OR PINCH PLEATS LOOK BEST ON WIDER DRAPERIES, SUCH AS THESE. THIS LOOK IS EASILY ACHIEVED USING THE CORRECT HEADING TAPE.

BELOW RIGHT: THESE ELEGANT CORNICES WITH A CLASSICAL GREEK KEY DESIGN CLEVERLY CONCEAL THE CURTAIN TRACKS.

Track options

choice	what	where
	Corded track is threaded with cords for automatic drawing of the draperies.	Best where it is difficult to reach the front edge of the draperies due to the positioning of furniture, or for very wide draperies.
	Curtain wire is a plastic-coated coiled wire with a screw hook at each end.	Threaded through curtains, it is hooked to a screw eye on the inside of the window frame. Only suitable for lightweight fabrics, though they can support heavier fabrics than tension rods.
	Double track is cleverly designed so that two tracks can be hung as one.	The perfect solution where you need one track for the valance and another for the draperies. Another use is where you want to hang sheers behind the main draperies.
	Tension rods are extendable and designed so they can be threaded through the tops of nets and sheers, automatically gathering the heading.	Fitted with an internal spring, tension rods can be wedged within the frame of the window. Only suitable for sheers of the lightest weight.
	Simple PVC track usually incorporates ring gliders to accommodate the drapery hooks. Can be bent into bays.	Suitable for hanging any drapery, whatever its weight.

Rods and finials

choice	what	where
	Brass rods are the all-time classic.	An excellent choice for living and dining rooms.
	Glass can be blown into fabulous shapes for finials.	This flame-like design works well on a brushed steel rod for an elegant modern look.
	Nickel is a popular metal for modern rods.	Not as strong as other metals, so usually reserved for lighter draperies. These lead crystal finials offer an architectural finish.
	Stainless steel is one of the strongest metals, so even the finer rods can support heavy draperies.	This simple light wood finial makes a sharp, contemporary statement.
	Wood is usually varnished for a natural look.	This antique French style with voluptuous turned finials has been painted for an ultra-chic look that would add elegance to any full-length draperies.
	Wrought iron is the traditional blacksmith's metal that combines strength with intricate finials, such as this traditional basket end.	A handsome and excellent choice for both traditional and contemporary homes.

Traditional valances and cornices offer a decorative way to conceal less than gorgeous rails, while adding interest to the tops of the draperies.

Valances, cornices, and swags and jabots

In the days when it was not fashionable to "express" the workings of architecture, the solution was to hide them. When it came to window treatments, the most beautiful solution was to hide curtain tracks and rods behind swags, cornices, and valances. These are still used, though they are mainly associated with period styles, and generally evoke the opulence and quality of yesteryear.

Valances Most look best when used to complement long draperies as they can look top-heavy over shorter curtains.

Cornices Traditionally made of painted wood, cornices can also be made from buckram, which is then covered with fabric that either matches or contrasts with the main draperies.

Swags and jabots date back to Federal times, making elegant dressings for their tall, slim windows. They are made up of fabric that is swagged across the top of the draperies plus a tailored strip that hangs down the sides, cut and folded to show off the contrasting lining on the reverse. Making them is best left to the professionals.

Swag and valance options

choice	what	where
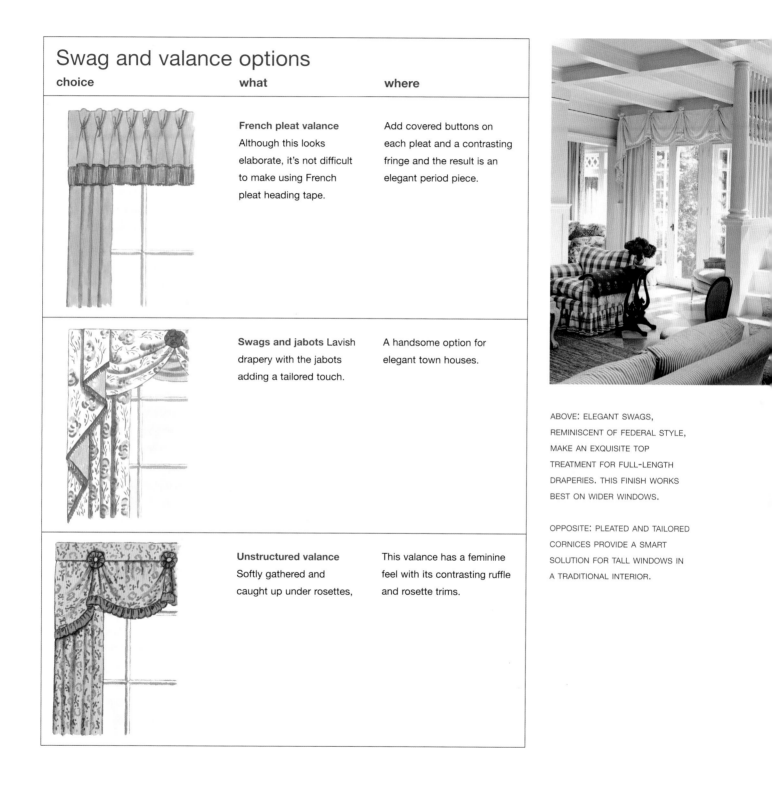	**French pleat valance** Although this looks elaborate, it's not difficult to make using French pleat heading tape.	Add covered buttons on each pleat and a contrasting fringe and the result is an elegant period piece.
	Swags and jabots Lavish drapery with the jabots adding a tailored touch.	A handsome option for elegant town houses.
	Unstructured valance Softly gathered and caught up under rosettes,	This valance has a feminine feel with its contrasting ruffle and rosette trims.

ABOVE: ELEGANT SWAGS, REMINISCENT OF FEDERAL STYLE, MAKE AN EXQUISITE TOP TREATMENT FOR FULL-LENGTH DRAPERIES. THIS FINISH WORKS BEST ON WIDER WINDOWS.

OPPOSITE: PLEATED AND TAILORED CORNICES PROVIDE A SMART SOLUTION FOR TALL WINDOWS IN A TRADITIONAL INTERIOR.

ACTION POINTS: using draperies

1 THINK DRAMA. THESE EXQUISITE FULL-LENGTH, ITALIAN-STRUNG DRAPERIES HAVE A SWAGGED HEADING THAT COULD ONLY BE MADE BY HAND. THEY ECHO THE FINE EMPIRE-LINE DRESSES THAT LADIES WORE IN THE EARLY EIGHTEENTH CENTURY.

2 ERR ON THE SIDE OF SIMPLICITY. AN ARCHITECTURAL FEATURE SUCH AS THIS FINE QUEEN ANNE-STYLE WINDOW NEEDS ONLY THE SIMPLEST OF WINDOW TREATMENTS. PLAIN WHITE DRAPERIES THAT ARE HUNG HIGH ABOVE THE WINDOW ARE THE PERFECT SOLUTION.

3 SHORT, ITALIAN-STRUNG STATIONARY DRAPERIES, COMPLETE WITH CORNICES, SOFTEN A WINDOW WITHOUT OVERWHELMING IT.

4 THE BURGUNDY EDGING ON THIS ELABORATE LAMBREQUIN (A CORNICE THAT EXTENDS DOWN THE SIDES OF THE WINDOW), ADDS A THEATRICAL AIR TO THESE WINDOWS.

Panels

If you're looking for a style that's simpler than traditional draperies, yet not as uncompromising as architectural shades (see pages 144–147), then panels could be the answer. Heading-free and very often no-sew into the bargain, they can be hung by tabs, ties, or clips on slender rods, or, minimally, tension wires. Alternatively, stretch panels onto frames and hang them at the window on a sliding track.

Freed from elaborate headings and tiebacks, panels complement, rather than envelop, the window architecture, yet have a softness that can't be offered by structured shades. The introduction of double- and triple-glazing and insulation means that people are dispensing with the heavier fabrics and going for lighter treatments.

Another appeal of panels is their economy of fabric, so you can afford to indulge in luxury, such as delicate organdies or laces, or finely embroidered silks from India.

Panels have a simplicity that adds a fresh modern feel to the interior.

Panels and their supports

choice	what	where
	**Clips and hooks** A small bulldog-style clip topped by a wire hook.	Designed for use with the lightest of sheers as its design complements delicate fabrics. Can be used on rods or tension wires.
	Clips with rings Another lightweight solution for sheers, though a little more robust than the hooked version.	Can be used as a complete window solution, or in conjunction with heavier draperies or in front of a Roman shade.
	**Grommets on tension wires** Do-it-yourself grommets are hammered through panel tops, then threaded onto tension wires or rods. For larger grommets, use a special grommet heading tape.	Best for medium-weight fabrics (sheers pull away from the grommet). Robust canvases and cotton weaves are a good choice for larger grommet styles. Whichever you choose, the result is fresh and modern.
	Shell wire clips Heavier-duty brass clips with scallop detailing inspired by antique equivalents.	Robust enough for heavier fabrics, the delightful detailing complements both traditional and contemporary window treatments. Ensure the rod is installed high enough above the window to avoid a light-gap between rod and fabric.

ABOVE: PANELS HUNG BY SIMPLE HOOKS ON WHITE RODS HAVE A SIMPLICITY THAT SUITS THE PURE MODERN DESIGN OF THIS CRISP DINING ROOM.

OPPOSITE: TRANSLUCENT PANELS LIKE THESE DRESS THE WINDOW WITHOUT CUTTING DOWN ON LIGHT TOO MUCH. IT'S THE PERFECT SOLUTION WHERE YOU ARE UNLIKELY TO BE EXPOSED TO PASSERSBY.

ACTION POINTS: using panels

1 COORDINATE PATTERNS. THE FRESH GREEN AND YELLOW STRIPES ON THESE TRANSLUCENT PANELS COMPLEMENT THE STRIPES OF THE PILLOWS, BRINGING A LIGHT TOUCH TO THE INTERIOR.

2 KEEP IT SIMPLE. THE BEAUTY OF A PLAIN WHITE PANEL CAN BE ENJOYED TO ITS FULL POTENTIAL WHEN THE HEADING IS LEFT UNADORNED.

3 TRY SOMETHING DIFFERENT. INSPIRED BY ALL THINGS NAUTICAL, THESE PANELS HAVE BEEN HUNG ONTO CURVED RODS USING CORD. IT'S AN EYECATCHING SOLUTION THAT IS ENHANCED BY THE CONTRASTING DEEP-TONED WALLS.

4 HERE, PANELS HAVE BEEN GIVEN A HEADING OF OUTSIZED GROMMETS THREADED ONTO A METAL ROD. IT'S AN IDEA BORROWED FROM RETAIL THAT WORKS WELL AT HOME.

Smart and
architectural,
structured
shades control
light efficiently
and enhance
pretty windows.

Structured shades

Chic and modern, structured shades always have an architectural feel to them. Fitted within the window frames, they complement, rather than conceal, the interior architecture. Even the most basic of structured shades are designed to use one or more various techniques designed to filter, let in, or block out the light, and this can have a bearing on the shades you choose.

Venetians made of slats These are still one of the most popular types. Made up of slats, they can be adjusted for light control, ranging from the closed position, which completely blocks out the light, to fully open, which provides a filter. They can also be raised to allow maximum light into the room, letting in even more than draperies, which tend to encroach a little onto the window panes.

Shades that roll up These range from the simplicity of roll-up paper shades to highly complex versions that can be made-to-measure in any shape to fit each individual pane. At the top end of the range, they can even be linked to automatic mechanisms for climate control.

Since structural shades need to fit the windows perfectly, size really does matter. Measuring has to be precise, and has to allow for any brackets or hardware. Most suppliers offer an on-site measuring service, a sensible option as shades that don't fit can then be re-made at their cost, rather than yours.

Your choice of shades will depend on both the style of the room and its particular needs for privacy and light filtration (see the options, opposite).
•**Where direct sunlight can dazzle** at certain times of the day, plan for the greatest flexibility, choosing shades such as Venetians or verticals that can quickly and easily be adjusted as needed.
•**North-facing rooms** that simply require privacy may be better furnished with shades made from a translucent material, from Japanese paper to high-tech modern reflective materials.

You may also like to consider whether to choose regular pull-down shades or those that pull up, protecting your privacy, while allowing sunlight to flood in from above.

1 THE NEUTRAL TONES OF FULL-WIDTH SPLIT CANE SHADES ADDS AN INEXPENSIVE MODERN LOOK TO THIS INTERIOR.

2 THESE TRANSLUCENT ROLLER SHADES SOFTEN THE VIEW, WHILE LETTING IN MOST OF THE LIGHT.

3 ROMAN SHADES ARE A CLASSIC WINDOW SOLUTION AND COMBINE WELL WITH OTHER DRESSINGS, SUCH AS DRAPERIES.

Structured shade options

choice	what	where
	**Matchstick blinds** Roll-up shades made from split cane, fine bamboo, or wooden strips. Offering no filtration, they work by a simple reefing system or an automatic roller mechanism.	Made from natural materials, these simple, inexpensive, and unpretentious shades look good in any interior that features natural materials.
	**Pleated** Made in modern translucent fabrics that are often treated with light-reflective coating. Can be made to any shape or size. Often made in powder-coated aluminum in a wide range of colors.	Smart, modern architectural interiors. Perfect where they are needed to color-match the walls.
	**Venetian** shades have adjustable slats in a range of widths that can be pierced with tiny holes or made with wavy edges for interesting light effects.	A neutral solution that works in both traditional and modern rooms.
	Vertical Vertical slats can be angled for quick and easy adjustments when needed; or pulled to one side for maximum daylight. Available in a wide range of textiles, aluminum, or PVC.	Traditionally associated with offices, these look fresh and modern in living rooms. Excellent where flexible light control is needed as they combine the benefits of both draperies and shades.

Soft shades
are a good
choice where
the window
architecture is
particularly
pleasing.

Soft shades

Ranging from sumptuously draped Austrian to plain-and-simple rolled, there's a soft shade to suit every decorative style. Softer than structured shades, they bring an element of drapery to the window.

Soft shades are pulled up by a variety of mechanisms:
- **Tied up** using simple ribbons
- **Pulled up by cords** threaded through rings at the back
- **A reefing system**
- **A spring-loaded roller.**

Most soft shades are made-to-measure, with each type using a different amount of fabric; gathered Austrians use the most and rollers the least. The flatter the shade, the more exacting its construction. The fabric needs to be cut exactly on the square to ensure it hangs correctly, and for some, such as Roman, working out how much fabric is needed and the position of the folds requires some meticulous mathematics. With all soft shades, beware of using striped fabric unless the repeat fits well within your window dimensions.

Soft shade options

choice	what	where
	**Austrian shades** with gathered frills are the ultimate pretty shade, offering all the textile advantages of drapes. Operated on a pulley system, have them made extra long to allow for draping, even when they're fully down.	Delightful in period homes (both city and country), depending on fabric choice. Best on larger windows.
	**Roller shades** are made from a panel of stiffened fabric cut to the size of the window frame. They can have a simple straight edge, or be finished with decorative braiding on a curved bottom edge.	Clean and unfussy, they look good in a modern interior. With a decorative bottom edge, they take on a more elegant, classic look.
	**Roman shades** pull up into crisp folds, supported by battens slipped between the lining and main fabric.	These classic shades always look elegant and work well in any interior. Excellent for a city apartment, especially if you like a modern look but prefer something softer than a structured solution.
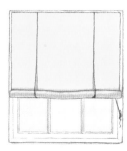	**Swedish shades** are made from unstiffened fabric, are usually lined, and operated by a simple pulley system.	Simple and unpretentious, these have an integrity that transcends time. Economical, they bring a fresh, pretty look to any window.

ABOVE: THESE DELIGHTFUL, TRANSLUCENT LONDON SHADES (AUSTRIAN SHADES MINUS THE TOP GATHERS) LOOK ELEGANT AND ETHEREAL IN THIS ROOM.

OPPOSITE: THIS PAIR OF STATIONARY LONDON SHADES WITH TAILS ADD SOFTNESS TO THE INTERIOR, LEAVING THE VENETIAN BLINDS THAT ARE BEHIND THEM TO DO THE WORK OF PRESERVING PRIVACY WHEN NEEDED.

Shutters

Traditionally part of the architecture of the windows, shutters were generally designed to deal with the local climate. So, in colder climates, where the night-time chill needed to be kept at bay, they were usually solid and paneled. During the day, when they were not needed, they were folded away neatly against the wall. In hotter climates, the challenge was to keep out the midday heat and glare, so shutters were generally louvered and often adjustable so they could be opened and closed as the sun moved around the house. Both offer good architectural solutions that are enduringly popular today and louvered shutters have become fashionable, even in cold climates. Shutters are still most commonly made of wood: paneled ones are often stripped and varnished or painted in a pale tone while louvered shutters are more likely to be painted in brighter colors, evoking the sunny climates that initially inspired their use.

OPPOSITE: PLANTATION SHUTTERS
ARE THE PERFECT WINDOW
DRESSING IN THIS ELEGANT
FEDERAL HOUSE. THEY ARE ALSO
SUPREMELY PRACTICAL AS EACH
SECTION OF LOUVERS CAN BE
OPENED AND SHUT SEPARATELY
FOR ULTIMATE LIGHT CONTROL.

LEFT: THESE PRETTY CURVE-
TOPPED WINDOWS ARE
COMPLEMENTED BY CUSTOM-
MADE SHUTTERS.

ACTION POINTS: using shades and shutters

1 SIMPLIFY LARGE WINDOWS. ROMAN SHADES MADE TO MATCH THE UPHOLSTERY CREATE A COHESIVE LOOK IN THIS LARGE LIVING ROOM.

2 PLAY UP THE ARCHITECTURE. PANELED BI-FOLD SHUTTERS COMPLEMENT PRETTY WINDOW SHAPES. THEY CAN BE PAINTED TO TEAM WITH ANY FUTURE REDECORATION OF THE ROOM.

3 USE WHITE TO BRIGHTEN. WHITE LONDON SHADES PROVIDE A CLASSIC SOLUTION IN ANY WELL-PROPORTIONED HOME.

4 CUSTOMIZE FOR PERFECT FIT. A CATHEDRAL WINDOW ARCH CAN BE A CHALLENGE, BUT BY CHOOSING LOUVERED SHUTTERS, THEY CAN MORE READILY BE CUSTOM MADE.

finishing touches

The finishing touches in a room are like the accessories of an outfit. The main pieces can be classic mainstays that stand the test of time, but the finishing touches add personal flair. In the home, they are chosen for many different reasons. Finishing touches may range from the simple and ephemeral, such as a vase of flowers, lasting only a few days, to something deeply meaningful and of sentimental value to the owner, such as a family painting that has been handed down through generations.

Finishing touches can also add a fashion element to the interior. While you may not want to change the colors of your walls, the upholstery, or flooring with great regularity, you may well be less daunted by the idea of updating the room with the addition of new pillows, vases, pictures, or flowers.

Turning a house into a home all comes down to adding a bit of yourself; indeed, a little bit of every member of the family. The finishing touches don't all have to be bought items; often the most beautiful and meaningful aren't.

Family photographs can evoke happy times and rites of passage: the birth of a new baby, first day at school, a wedding, vacation, or even just a special moment. Children's paintings, too, well framed, can look very striking. Or you may decide to frame some autumn leaves, acorns, or pretty pebbles collected on a day out in the country, all of which can be made into wonderful displays.

But for the most part, we think of the finishing touches as lamps, pillows, rugs, wall mirrors, vases, and bowls, and many of these can be changed relatively inexpensively if you want to update the room without going to the trouble of complete redecoration. Just as with the sentimental belongings and ephemera, the key to the finishing touches comes down to the display. It doesn't matter whether your style is minimal modern or country comfy, it's what you do with what you have that counts.

ABOVE: FRESH SEASONAL FLOWERS GIVE LIFE TO AN INTERIOR, CREATING A NEW LOOK WEEK AFTER WEEK AS YOU SUBSTITUTE NEW ARRANGEMENTS.

OPPOSITE: EVEN IN A WHITE-ON-WHITE ROOM, THE FINISHING TOUCHES ADD PERSONALITY AND FLAIR. A ROW OF TAILORED CUSHIONS, A TRIO OF GILT-FRAMED DRAWINGS, BLOSSOMING TWIGS, AND A SHAPELY VASE TURN A SIMPLE CORNER INTO AN INVITING SPACE.

THE MOST FASCINATING DISPLAYS
OFFER GLIMPSES OF OUR LIVES.
THESE ARTIFACTS, COLLECTED
OVER SEVERAL JOURNEYS, ARE
EXQUISITELY DISPLAYED. THE
SCALE OF THE ARTIFACTS RELATES
PERFECTLY TO THE SHELVES.

Paintings need to relate to the scale and proportions of the wall on which they are hung. So either choose a picture that fills the whole space, or arrange several to make a pleasing group. You may link them by color or by the way in which they are framed. You may hang a series in matching sizes and frames in ordered ranks, or you may create a jigsaw of several favorites. Small, detailed works need to be hung on small areas of wall and where you are likely to be looking at them close up, such as near a doorway you regularly pass through. Another tip is to hang them at about eye level. In a sitting room, this may well mean eye level when you're sitting down.

Lamps are often chosen almost as a piece of sculpture, adding stature and form to the whole interior. Bear this in mind when buying: you may well, for example, buy a pair, to make a statement at either end of a console table.

Pillows can have a huge influence on the whole interior. The contribution they make to the overall color scheme is one obvious reason. Many people prefer to choose muted or neutral shades for their upholstery so that it doesn't date, then scatter pillows to add color, even swapping them in summer and winter. For a strong look, buy them as groups in either matching or complementary tones. However, color is only one influence pillows have on the interior. Their size and how they are trimmed also has a huge bearing on their overall effect. Subtly piped cushions, for example, look tailored; if they're big, squashy, floral, and ruffled, the look is more country.

Vases and flowers When it comes to these, use similar principles to those of displaying pictures: small arrangements on small shelves, for example, and huge, floor-based arrangements in large halls or by the fireplace. For table arrangements, either use a single vase that relates to the scale of the table, group a pair, or set several in a row on longer surfaces, such as down the length of a refectory table.

1 A FOURSOME OF ALUMINUM CONTAINERS LINK SPRING BULBS AND CUT FLOWERS, MAKING AN ENCHANTING DISPLAY.

2 A BOLD CHINA COLLECTION CREATES IMPACT WHEN TIGHTLY GROUPED ONTO ACLOVE SHELVES, AS HERE.

3 A DISPLAY OF OTHERWISE DISPARATE OBJECTS IS UNIFIED BY THE FACT THAT THEY ARE ALL MADE OF GLASS.

4 A ROW OF HANDSOME GOLD PILLOWS ADD A SENSE OF GRANDEUR TO A SIMPLE WHITE-PAINTED SWEDISH BENCH.

ACTION POINTS: finishing touches

1 THINK BIG. PHOTOGRAPHIC IMAGING MAKES STRIKING DISPLAYS EVER MORE ATTAINABLE. HERE, 36 PANELS FORM A HUGE PICTURE THAT BRINGS FOCAL IMPACT TO A SIMPLE ROOM.

2 MATCH COLORS. WHEN YOU HAVE A DISPARATE COLLECTION, LINK THE ITEMS WITH SCALE AND COLOR. ALTHOUGH THE SHELLS AND CORALS HAVE A SEASIDE THEME, THE SCULPTURES DON'T LOOK OUT OF PLACE BECAUSE THEY HAVE A SIMILAR SCALE AND TONE.

3 GROUP SIMILAR ITEMS. LINK A GROUP OF PICTURES OF DIFFERENT SIZES BY THEIR COLOR AND FRAMES. TOGETHER THEY WILL THEN MAKE AN IMPRESSIVE DISPLAY.

4 ADD A NATURAL TOUCH. USE FLOWERS TO ADD PERSONALITY AND CHARM TO A ROOM. HERE, AN ARMFUL OF SUMMER FLOWERS HAS BEEN PACKED INTO A BLUE FLOWER BUCKET TO DO JUST THAT.

PHOTOGRAPHY CREDITS

The publisher would like to thank the following photographers for supplying the pictures in this book:
(**b** = bottom, **c** = center, **l** = left, **r** = right, **t** = top)

Page 1 Laura Moss; **2** Tim Street-Porter; **3** Carlos Domenech; **4** Victoria Pearson; **6** Ellen McDermott; **7** Don Freeman; **8** Roger Davies; **10** Eric Piasecki; **11** William Waldron; **12** Dominique Vorillon; **13** Simon Upton; **14** Polly Eltes; **15** Anthony Cotsifas; **16 l** Erik Kvalsvik; **16 r** Carlos Domenech; **17** Simon Upton; **18** William Waldron; **19** Brendan Paul; **20 l** Jonn Coolidge; **20 r** Tria Giovan; **21** Tria Giovan; **22** Scott Frances; **23** Oberto Gili; **24** Jonn Coolidge; **26** Jonn Coolidge; **27** Oberto Gili; **29 tl** Vicente Wolf; **29 tr** Tria Giovan; **29 bl** Jonn Coolidge; **29 br** Oberto Gili; **30 l** Roger Davies; **30 c** Erik Kvalsvik; **30 r** Tim Beddow; **33** Firooz Zahedi; **34** Carlos Domenech; **36** Charles Maraia; **37** Paul Warchol; **38** Don Freeman; **39 tl** Simon Upton; **39 tr** Grey Crawford; **39 bl** Brendan Paul; **39 br** Antoine Bootz; **40** Roger Davies; **43** Antoine Bootz; **45 t** Gordon Beall; **45 c** Eric Piasecki; **45 b** Karyn Millet; **47** William Waldron; **48** Vicente Wolf; **49 t** Jonn Coolidge; **49 bl** John Gould Bessler; **49 br** Tim Street-Porter; **50** Simon Upton; **51** Tria Giovan; **53 tl** Jonn Coolidge; **53 tr** Eric Piasecki; **53 bl** Jonn Coolidge; **53 br** Tim Street-Porter; **55 t** Jonn Coolidge; **55 c** Simon Upton; **55 b** Simon Upton; **56** Laura Moss; **58** Roger Davies; **59 t** Tria Giovan; **59 bl** Simon Upton; **59 br** Peter Margonelli; **60 t** Oberto Gili; **60 c** Eric Piasecki; **60 b** William Waldron; **62** Jonn Coolidge; **64** Gordon Beall; **65 t** Roger Davies; **65 bl** Jonn Coolidge; **65 br** Colleen Duffley; **66** Grey Crawford; **67 t** Gordon Beall; **67 bl** Oberto Gili; **67 br** Grey Crawford; **68** Victoria Pearson; **69** Tria Giovan; **70** Jonn Coolidge; **71 tl** Tim Street-Porter; **71 tr** Dominique Vorillon; **71 bl** Simon Upton; **71 br** Laura Moss; **72** Victoria Pearson; **73** Paul Whicheloe; **74** Jonn Coolidge; **75 t** Oberto Gili; **75 bl** Jonn Coolidge; **75 br** Fernando Bengoechea; **76** Vicente Wolf; **78** Eric Boman; **79 t** Eric Piasecki; **79 bl** Tim Beddow; **79 br** Jonn Coolidge; **80** Luke White; **81** Dominique Vorillon; **82** John Bamber; **84** Victoria Pearson; **85 t** William Waldron; **85 bl** Victoria Pearson; **85 br** Laura Moss; **86 t** Victoria Pearson; **86 c** Simon Upton; **86 b** John M Hall; **88** Tria Giovan; **89 t** Jonn Coolidge; **89 bl** Jeff McNamara; **89 br** Christopher Baker; **90** Oberto Gili; **92** Victoria Pearson; **93 t** Jonn Coolidge; **93 b** Jonn Coolidge; **94** Tria Giovan; **95** William Waldron; **96 t** Eric Piasecki; **96 b** Susan Gentry McWhinney; **98** Tim Street-Porter; **99** Oberto Gili; **100** Gordon Beall; **101 t** Edmund Barr; **101 bl** Gordon Beall; **101 br** Eric Piasecki; **102** Tim Street-Porter; **103 t** Luca Trovato; **103 bl** Tria Giovan; **103 br** Oberto Gili; **104** Eric Piasecki; **105 t** Dana Gallagher; **105 bl** Victoria Pearson; **105 br** Carlos Domenech; **106** Roger Davies; **107 t** Jeff McNamara; **107 bl** Pieter Estersohn; **107 br** Carlos Domenech; **108** Hugh Stewart; **109** Antoine Bootz; **110** Hugh Stewart; **111** Grey Crawford; **112** Karyn Millet; **113 t** Jonn Coolidge; **113 bl** Jonn Coolidge; **113 br** William Waldron; **114** Dana Gallagher; **115** Jonn Coolidge; **116 l** Simon Upton; **116 r** Jeremy Samuelson; **117** Susan Gilmore; **118** Ellen McDermott; **119 t** Francois Dischinger; **119 bl** Fernando Bengoechea; **119 br** Oberto Gili; **120** Christopher Simon Sykes; **121** Eric Roth; **122** Eric Roth; **123** Tria Giovan; **124** Roger Davies; **125 t** Simon Upton; **125 bl** Andreas von Einsiedel; **125 br** Jack Thompson; **126** Carlos Emilio; **127** Fernando Bengoechea; **128** Christopher Baker; **129** Jeremy Samuelson; **130** Roger Davies; **131 t** Christopher Baker; **131 c** Eric Piasecki; **131 b** Antoine Bootz; **132** Joshua McHugh; **133 l** Bruce Buck; **133 r** William Waldron; **136** Tim Street-Porter; **137** Oberto Gili; **138** Gordon Beall; **139 t** Tim Street-Porter; **139 bl** Tria Giovan; **139 br** Oberto Gili; **140** Dana Gallagher; **142** Dana Gallagher; **143 t** Eric Piasecki; **143 bl** Oberto Gili; **143 br** Christopher Baker; **145 t** Dominique Vorillon; **145 c** Roger Davies; **145 b** Roger Davies; **146** Tria Giovan; **147** Antoine Bootz; **148** Eric Boman; **149** Gordon Beall; **150** Grey Crawford; **151** Carlos Domenech; **151 top** Roger Davies; **151 bl** Roger Davies; **151 br** Oberto Gili; **152** Laura Moss; **153** Carlos Domenech; **154** Dominique Vorillon; **155 tl** Ellen McDermott; **155 tr** Jim Bastardo; **155 bl** Laura Resen; **155 br** Tria Giovan; **156** Dominique Vorillon; **157 t** Don Freeman; **157 bl** Jonn Coolidge; **157 br** Eric Boman.

INDEX

Page numbers in *italics* refer to
illustrations.

A

accent colors 96, *101*
accent lighting 40
activities 16, 28
alcoves 68, 70, *154*
architecture 28, 40, 52, *71*,
110
armoires *72*
Art Nouveau 42, 46

B

bamboo flooring 56
bookcases *71*
brick floors *51*, 54
buffets *70*, 77
built-in furniture 28, 68–70, *71*,
74–75

C

cabinets 22, 68, *69, 71, 73*,
76, 79, 96
carpentry 28
carpet 28, 50, 60–61, *65, 67*
   squares 50, 60, *67*
ceiling 114, *117, 118*
ceiling lights 45
ceramic tiles 50, 52, 54, *58*
chairs, easy 80, 83
   see also dining chairs
chaise longue 83
chandeliers 40, 44, 45
clay tiles and bricks *53*, 54
closets 22, 68
coffee tables *27*, 82, 85
coir 62, *62–63*
Colonial style 70, 98, 122
color 13, *79*, 92, 93, *94–107*

bright *94*, 98–99
contrast *96*, 98
finishing touches 154, *157*
flooring 50, *58, 59, 67*
harmonizing *95*, 96, 98
paint 114
upholstery 82, *93, 94*
color wheel 94, 97
console tables *22*, 77, 154
cornices 136, *139*
coves 40
cupboards *69*, 70

D

decorating checklist 93
decorative lighting 40, 42, 44
diffused light 38, 43
digital imaging 120
dimmer switches 38, 40
dining chairs 80, 86–87, *86, 107*
   folding/stacking 22, 80, 86, 87
   slipcovers 86, *112*
dining rooms 20–25
   furniture 20, 80, 86–89
   lighting and electricity *39*,
   44–7, 48
   multifunction *17*, 22
   single-use 20–21
   storage 20–21, *69, 70*,
   76–79
dining table *20, 22*, 80, 86,
88–89
direct/indirect light 38, 43, *45*
display 152, *154, 157*
   space 18, *73, 75*, 76,
doors 18, 25, 28, 70–73, *71*
downlights, recessed 36, *37*,
   38, *39*, 40, 41, 44
drafting lamps 42
draperies 92, 126, 128–139

headings 130, 131
rods/finials 128, 130, 135
swags and valances 136–137
tapes and hooks 133
tracks 128, 130, 133–134
yardage 130

E

electricity 40, 44, *49*
   outlets 26, 28, *29*, 44

F

fabric 13, 93, 97, 108
   draperies 130
   panels 25, 92, 126, 140–143
   wall coverings 120
feature lighting 40
Federal-style: fireplace 31
   lighting 46, *47*
   storage 70
   walls 98, *120, 122*
   windows 126, 136, *148*
file, information 13, 92
finials 128, 135
finishing touches 93, 152–157
fireplace *10*, 28, *29*, 30–31
floors 28, 50–67
   hard 28, 50, 52–59
   soft 50, 60–65
flowers 152, 154, *155, 157*
focal point *85*, 110
   fireplace 28, *29*, 30, 85
   lighting 40, 41, 44, 45
   television *10, 19*
function 14, 16, 18, 22
furniture 26, 28, 80–89
   built-in 28
   dining room 20, 22, 80, 86–89
   living room 80, 82–85
   made-to-measure *27*

positioning 33, 82, 85
storage *68, 70, 71*, 72

G, H

geometrics 108, 116, 130
   carpets *60, 65, 110*
granite floors 54
heating 22, 28, 30–32
holdbacks 128
home theater 14, 16, 18, 28
   electrical outlets 44
   positioning 33

J, K, L

jute 62, 65
lamps 38, 40, 42, 44, *49*, 154
layout 26–34
lifestyle 14–16
light 18, *18, 22*, 110, *140*
lighting 36–49
   dining room 44–47
   living room 40–44
   types 38–40
   wiring 40
limestone floors 54
living-dining room 18, *22–25*,
   24–25
   flooring 52, 60
   lighting 36, *48*
   screening 25
   storage *22*
living rooms 18
   furniture 80, 82–85
   lighting and electricity 40–44
   positioning furniture 33–34
   storage 16, 18, 34, *68*, 73–75

M

marble floors *53*, 54
mirrors 152